Sew What!? How to Design Sustainable Fashion

Vol.1   The Basics

Dinie van den Heuvel

d'andt

Selfpublished in Belgium by d'andt. www.dinievandenheuvel.com

Book Cover by Grimaud Leclercq   Illustrations by Grimaud Leclercq

A CIP catalogue record for this book is available from the Belgian National Liberary.

ISBN 9789464755701 English hardcover. ISBN 9789464755718 English paperback.

For Mauritz,

who deserves the best possible world, for real!

Contents

Concepts must be value-based

Inspire optimism

Blank canvas

A particular state of mind

Design thinking

Character

Perseverance

Empathy

Humility

Understanding strength in numbers

Creative confidence

Manufacturing trials

Failure and error

Ecological literacy and respect for locality

The power of storytelling

Criteria

Design tools

Books

Articles

Reports

Documentary

One

Introduction

F OR MANY YEARS FASHION has lived a fairy tale reading of the world. In Voltaire's 1759 satire *Candide*, the eponymous protagonist accepts the world as it is, no matter the suffering, pain, and evil inherent in it. It is *le meilleur des mondes possible*, the best of all possible worlds, and in accepting it, Candide is relieved of any responsibility for harm he causes or witnesses. It simply is supposed to be this way.

As the world exists like this, and as it is already the best possible version, there is no need to intervene or strive to do better. It makes mysterious beauty and intangible luxury and needs no further questioning, just indulgence.

Unfortunately, it is this very allegory of systematic blindness that we practice when it comes to what fashion produces: we don't know and don't see many things. We do not feel responsible for the pain, destruction and suffering fashion entails.

The spell that the fashion industry has cast urgently needs to be broken. As with Narcissus who fell in love with his own reflection, fashion today is in love with itself, operating in a vacuum, mesmerised, and enthralled by the beauty it creates.

Over the past 20 years, more and more cracks have appeared in the illusion: stories have emerged about the abuse, pollution and violence hidden behind the veil of pretty clothes. Those working inside the industry have their suspicions about how things are being made and are aware that the shroud obscures what should not be allowed to happen. Every so often, that veil is pushed aside, allowing us a glimpse of what lies beyond: notes are found in fast fashion pieces with cries for help.

Around the world, Covid lockdowns resulted in a loss of customers for so many production companies and no financial support existed to take care of their workers. Documentaries released showing garbage being dumped in waterways, misconduct in factories, harassment of young people finding their way in our industry. It is tempting to discard each story as an anecdote, and thus to uphold the ideal of abundance, limited only by our own creativity and ingenuity. Many are happy to close their eyes to it all, to remain blind and blissfully unaware of the pain and suffering, only seeing the mysterious glow of fashion.

Some claim that this is what the public wants: a moment to escape and dream, mesmerised by these little pieces of craftsmanship, hidden behind a veil that playfully exposes only what is chosen to be revealed.

This is the Voltaire joke, and the joke is on us.

However, the joke is not the striving for abundance, or the limitless belief in our own creativity and ingenuity. The joke is that we have refused to acknowledge the impact our actions and ideas have. Our actions are never limitless, never without consequence. We might choose to ignore them, but their impact remains unaltered.

The simple act of accepting the impact of each action, combined with human creativity and a desire to create, might lead us out of the shadows and into the light. I would argue that the fashion world today contains immense suffering, too great to justify the belief that we created the "best of all possible worlds". But it is exactly this that we could and should re-*create*: we have the power to design the world of tomorrow as we envision it. It is time to aim at making our industry truly the best of all possible versions of itself. We must investigate its dark sewers and redesign them bathed in the sunlight.

The first time I knew I wanted to work in fashion, I was 11 years old. In school we had learned how to make a doll, and a helpful mother explained to me how to measure my finished toy, translate the numbers in some magical way, use the data to draw a geometrical shape, and just like that, it morphed into a gown for my doll.

A sense of delight battled with the fascination about the transition happening in front of me. How could some random numbers, some flat shape become a three-dimensional dress? It felt like magic to me. That day, I got home and begged my mother for a piece of cloth, determined to use that same process to make me a dress.

It was my first realisation that the clothes I owned were made by a simple process of measuring, cutting, and sewing. That day, the sky became the limit.

My career has led me many places, but it always brought me back to one fundamental understanding: that with perseverance and research, any dress could materialise, and that I or somebody else could make it.

Many years – and dresses – later I still feel amazed that I can make something, create something that did not exist before I started, and will be useable once I'm done. When talking to other designers they often recall a similar moment of fascination and excitement, that determined their professional path, and that sensation is what they are still after to this day.

Along my sustainable fashion journey, my fashion label, Infantium Victoria, has been an invaluable tool. It is a testing ground for my thoughts and ideas, living proof that it is possible to design with freedom and creativity, while still aiming to be completely and absolutely human- and planet friendly. The reaction I encounter most when talking about sustainable fashion design, is from designers sighing about how being sustainable limits their creativity; it is nice to show them how at Infantium Victoria, we turn those limits into opportunities and creative challenges.

I was introduced to ideas about design thinking early on in my career, and it is my personal experience that the *tools* to think about any problem remain more or less the same, regardless of the problem at hand. The more you practice problem solving, the better the outcome of your process, every time you apply it. Finding solutions is a skill anybody can develop: the most important requirement is that you are aware of the problem that exists.

Today, humankind is facing tremendous problems. In 2019, the Intergovernmental Panel on Climate Change (IPCC), declared that climate change is widespread, rapid, and intensifying. The window in which we might avert catastrophic climate change is closing rapidly. The problems we are facing are created by human-doing, and it is up to us to find ways to stop and hopefully reverse this.

In fashion, we grew accustomed to uninterrupted growth and a system that has only served small parts of our communities, while leaving the majority of people in the supply chain in utter poverty.

It is worth asking if your design skills are best used to create just another mesmerising dress, or if they would be better directed towards creating a disruptive new way of doing things within our industry. Man-made systems, practices, and objects do not evolve by accident. They mostly change because somebody identified something they no longer wanted to support, and they focused on designing and realising their desired alternative. And sometimes these things evolve because an accident occurred and someone was clever enough to see the advantage of this new shape, way or form and decided to keep it, and maybe even multiply and optimise it.

Change will need to be dramatic, frame shifting, and a true transformation. And it will hurt. Mostly for the people that profited from the existing system for so long, who got rich at the expense of the planet and the other, who will have to learn to do with less.

But the alternative is inconceivable. If we don't do anything, all of humankind will be hurt, as well as every living being on this planet. If we continue to close our eyes, believe in the fairy tale that all will be fine, the planet will survive, but for its inhabitants the future will be much less secure.

For me the transition towards sustainable fashion practice has been both fast and slow. Some changes happened so gradually that I didn't even notice my own practice evolving; others happened radically and overnight. Some much needed changes in my own practice I identified early on in my career, but have been an ongoing struggle for the better part of the last 20 years to realise.

During my teaching years, I have witnessed first-hand the confrontation between young idealistic fashion designers and the fashion industry. And it leaves a lot to be desired.

Problems start early on in the education system: in each school, I encounter at least one student who is passionate about the environment, about animal welfare, about doing things differently, in a collective, using castoff materials, all these things that we have catalogued for a long time as green thinking.

I have sat in conversations with these students where they try to explain their values to their coaches and other tutors. They talk about their dreams, their vision, about how they believe our fashion industry could and should develop its clothing. What practices are good practices.

These students are not formally educated on this topic, yet they speak with passion and conviction. They have the youthful naivete that they will change the world, and they are not limited as yet by the reality of how the fashion industry imposes its ways. How it is very hard to change methods that are so massively embedded in the cross-over of an industry. Often, the education system fails to give these young, ambitious, game-changers the tools to define and realise their ideal fashion world.

Recently, I interviewed a prospective intern and asked them why they where interested in our company. I had received their portfolio and noticed an abundance of plastic, PUR foam, and other oil products. So, what had inspired this student to come knocking on our door? After all, I lead a sustainable, vegan, organic fashion brand, and I teach on the topic in many institutions. One might even consider me an optimistic advocate for radical ground-shifting change.

They glanced at me, shook their head, and looked down. Then, they explained how enthusiastically they had started their studies. How inspired they were to make environmentally good choices. How this had been something they had learned as a small child, and until today, had kept as a guiding principle. They did not really understand what had happened during the time they did their bachelor's degree, but sometime in the first few weeks, the teaching team managed to convince them that design required a complete freedom from restrictions, and that values and principles were limiting to one's development. They intimated that if you didn't let go of such concepts, you might never achieve greatness as a designer.

For the past 30 years or so, fashion schools around the globe have been teaching their students how to design clothes. The program in each school has different features, but in general, students learn to draw, to make patterns, to sew. They are taught fashion history and art history, and they learn how to create their personal creative universe. Vital to this process is that designers learn to interpret the Zeitgeist: what is operating in society today, and how to anticipate what should be worn tomorrow. But for the longest time, the question of sustainability or personal moral compass was not considered a key starting point.

The holy grail of fashion design seems to be to freely experiment with volume in space. To be freed of all restrictions. Only in this manner could everything and anything ignite an idea. The call for sustainability, in any form, might create limitations and highlight the road to be travelled, and in so doing, it would impose elements or choices, thus hindering the endless freedom a fashion designer needs to create greatness. In this chain of thought, sustainability needs to be merely an issue for the production team. The technical team in charge of producing clothes should be concerned about altering the design into something sustainable, but it has no place in the design process.

This has been a position I encounter repeatedly, and in many different schools and companies, expressed in various ways by well-intentioned fashion professionals. I've witnessed fashion houses and brands where the sustainability question is discussed and evaluated by separate departments, far away from its designers.

Somehow it does not make any sense.

And it did not make sense to the young student sitting across from me, hoping for an internship position.

The thought of dismissing sustainability as a technical problem, to be solved by technicians keeps designers liberated from taking responsibility for their creations. But the impact of any design is at the core of its design; not something to be solved by an engineer afterwards.

Fashion designers should be accountable for their ideas and creations, not just the visual part, but all other aspects too. The quality and origin of the materials that are used, the life after its current form, the people who participated in the making, the well-being of all living beings who came across the creation. The waste it creates and how to create a positive impact are all topics designers should question and formulate answers to. Only in this way, can designers be truly engaged in designing their world of tomorrow.

This book is not about how to learn to design. There are excellent schools for this, with many different approaches.

But in a way it *is* about how to design.

I will argue that to create creative yet sustainable designs you cannot develop one after another.

This means one should not assume that a creative universe can be constructed, garments can be drawn and made and at the end the sustainable sauce can be added.

It does not work like this.

Thinking about design and sustainability should happen simultaneously against a backdrop of the values you wish to uphold.

Change in your practice is a process, handling one issue at a time. It is my wish to share the tools to question and change your thinking about fashion design. I encourage everyone to find their own way to implement sustainable design thinking within their values and design ideals.

There is no one perfect way. It helps if a value framework is constructed. If you externalise your value framework it will help you find your sustainable path, guide your decisions, without limiting your creative freedom. If you find your own way to implement and master sustainable design thinking, limitless creative satisfaction becomes a possibility.

The solutions and systems we employed till date have resulted in our current problems. Relying entirely on them for change will not work. New systems need to be designed and used to accelerate and shift our future. Any system that seeks to direct us away from the devastating road we are on, will need to place our natural resources and respect for our planet at its core.

After all, it is our planet that provides for all we have.

When you define your way, it will be your voice, therefore making it more powerful than anything governments, your boss, or anybody else could ever impose on you. And it will make you feel part of something greater. The ideals and values will guide practices that can change our industry to become a pure power for good, establishing better lives for all those that directly and indirectly work with or for you. A brighter and safer planet for all of us, and the generations to come, and the gratification that you, intentionally, with your limitless creativity have contributed in a vital way, to creating positive impact on everything surrounding you.

It is my wish to inspire you to look at what is and envision the future you want to be part of. Step by step, it can become reality. One dress at a time.

On the topic of restraint there is still a lot to be said, and throughout the book, we will address this from different angles. At this point I do want to highlight that it is a fact of fashion that it deals with restrictions. It dresses a body, protects it from the elements, expresses personal choices. The restraint some people refer to when talking about sustainable design are, for me, just as fundamental as the previous three restraints.

All these restraints are a fundamental element of what it means to design fashion. It is a product, a commodity, an object of desire, all at once. At the end of the day, fashion is applied art. It produces a product to be worn by a body. Fashion and clothing might help one connect and experience the elements, and they have the power to spark joy. The restraint of sustainability must become as inherently a part of fashion as the restraint to dress a body.

If recent times have shown the world anything, it is that the younger generations are ready to fight for their future, that as a group anything is possible, and I like to believe that nobody willingly intends to destroy our planet. We need awareness and a will to make a new reality our reality. I hope that I will inspire you to think, question and hopefully change your thoughts, methods, and practices.

After 20 years I still love fashion, even with all its ugly sides. Only by recognising them, acknowledging the reality of today is change possible.

I know it's scary, and we don't know what a new reality should look like. Yet, I am inviting you on a journey, so travel along and let's start designing something new.

For a designer, what could possibly be more exciting?

Two

A value framework for guidance

P EOPLE OFTEN ASK ME how it all began.

Every time this question is posed, I hesitate to answer. What drives me to design an award-winning "green" sustainable children's clothing collection?

The truth is, I owe a big part of my thinking and norms to my upbringing. I learned at an early age not to take anything for granted, that responsibility goes much further than the eye can see, and, that all of this is simple – though not easy – if you know what to do.

It requires genuine commitment: you must be prepared to accept the consequent actions generated by your beliefs.

I started working in fashion for a high-end independent fashion brand where I observed, learned, and played in the fashion field. We made gorgeous clothes designed to make you feel different when you wore them. The clothes empowered the wearer. It was, and remains, a transformative feeling to wear the pieces my then-boss designed.

Being in a small company gave me the opportunity to observe up close the struggles to find manufacturers, to get ideas realized, to involve our audience in our visions.

I left the first brand I worked for after two years. After studying and an apprenticeship I started on my own, working for various brands and designers. Over time, I started seeing the underlying, unaddressed structural problems of the fashion industry: overproduction, bad materials and choices often made based solely on what was nice and easy and nothing else. It was not even about aesthetics since that would require functionality and construction to exist in harmony.

Then, about 15 years ago, I started exploring more sustainable practices. I opened a uniform company investigating what the best solution would be for every customer. I challenged the design demands simultaneously with the production processes involved.

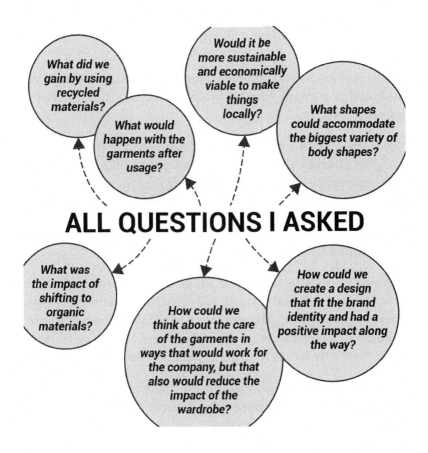

Simple not easy

The exercise we performed for our customers taught me that there are many ways of being less bad and, even good sometimes. And that choosing the right path for my customer did not devalue other paths taken by other customers. It simply meant choosing what fitted best with their specific values, needs, and demands.

Working for various companies, watching them choose and define their non-negotiables finally lead me to formulate my own values and beliefs. To search for my preferred ways of designing and making clothes within my value framework.

When Julia, my current business partner came along, we quickly figured out that we shared beliefs about good practices and about sustainable clothing and that we both had a strong desire to create clothing without compromising our convictions.

We started our brand, and never settled for less than our ideals.

Every new season we learn about new problems, which we refer to as "challenges", and we start addressing them. Investigating the current situation, looking for alternatives, and researching the found potential solutions. By nature, I have a suspicious little voice at the back of my head that challenges most of what I know and an insatiable desire to understand things around me. Even something as simple as decaffeinated coffee can spark my curiosity! How do you get caffeine out of a bean? Is it still a wholesome product? Or is it become something engineered into something I would rather not consume?[1]

So, let's look deeper into this.

There is no easy way out. If you bought this book, hoping for an easy fix, I'll be straight with you: there is no easy fix.

Those that claim they have found easy solutions, I guarantee you, did not change their thinking, their beliefs, and their practices. They simply added a Band-Aid to their normal procedures, known today as "green washing". They dipped their work in another layer of ob-fuscation, polluting our minds and our world. But we don't want to dwell too much on this. After all, this is not what interests me; it is not what I want to talk about. And frankly, it is not my expertise.

So how is sustainable design simple?

Simple means that once you identify your values and beliefs, the consequences will be crystal clear in front of you. Simple guidelines that will realize your dreams and ideals. Simple steps to take. Simple procedures to follow. Simple questions each of us should think about and formulate answers to, for everything we design. That isn't easy by any means.

---

1. For those curious souls like me: there are four main methods to extract caffeine from a coffee bean. All of them rely on soaking the green bean, either in water or in a solvent (usually methylene chloride or ethyl acetate) and then blasted with CO_2 to draw out the caffeine. The first successful extraction of caffeine used benzene, but since this is a known carcinogen, this technique was quickly abandoned. It sounds rather unappealing, coffee soaked in chemicals, but not all chemicals are bad. Technically speaking, everything around us is a chemical. The methylene chloride residue in the beans is essentially non-existent and eth-yl acetate is a natural fruit usually made from acetic acid, the main building block of vinegar. The liquid CO_2 only attaches to caffeine molecules, drawing them out of the unroasted beans. The gas is easily removed once the pressure is removed.

As a general premise we human beings are united in a common value: we do not wish to cause intentional harm to others or to the world.

So, a key question is: "How can one design or manufacture in a way that loves all children, of all species, for all time?"[2]

This is vital and the principle reoccurring question that needs answering at every step of the way. How can you design your garments to be economically viable, aesthetically pleasing, *and* good for all time? This is my benchmark question, the one question that either greenlights my idea, or sends me back to the drawing board.

Choice is a decision

Design and fashion design are constantly confronted by constraints. Constraints of the body you are dressing and the freedom of movement you want to grant your wearer. Constraints of the materials you are choosing, of colours you are using. Each choice you make eliminates all other options, for this particular garment or process. In a way designing is making choices, all the time.

If we add the question of ethics to the way we design and realize our garments, this becomes just another choice with its associated implications.

Just as choosing to make a black garment excluded all other colours at that point, choosing to make this dress locally excludes all other production locations. However, it says nothing about all the other dresses you will make in your life. It only influences this specific object.

---

2. William McDonough & Michael Braungart, The Upcycle: Beyond Sustainability – Designing for Abundance (New York: North Point Press, 2013) pg.9

Each new collection, each new object, all your choices are open again, requiring decisions. Decisions that you make based on the information you have collected and values you want to uphold.

Why not willingly accept your value framework as just another constraint? Then, dealing with ethical constraints becomes a design challenge for you to creatively tackle over and over. For which you are challenged to formulate an answer, embedded in the design.

Until recently, process and product responsibility were not something actively considered by fashion designers. To practice sustainable design, one needs to accept full responsibility of the product you are making, and how you are making it. And why not see it as a challenge to make it the best possible way you know how?

For my brand we have done some things in the past; which today, with the knowledge I have gathered, I would have done differently. This does not mean they were a bad choice, or a bad product. It simply means I used my available knowledge and value framework at that specific time to make the best possible decisions available to me. Choices made with the right intentions and using all the available information at that time might still turn out to be wrong in the future. We cannot do more than be sincere, ask questions as we collect as much information as possible so as to make the best possible decision in any given moment.

Asking with intent

William McDonough and Michael Braungart wrote a book entitled *The Upcycle,*[3] in which they emphasize how important *intention* is, this is what gets you started. It helps battle the feeling of being overwhelmed.

---

3. William McDonough & Michael Braungart, The Upcycle: Beyond Sustainability – Designing for Abundance, pg. 215

Many people working in fashion today feel paralyzed by this seemingly new demand for sustainable practices. There are no rules, and there is very little defined of what the demand for sustainability even means.

If you embrace the idea that intention is important, and that getting started is the only way to improve, every action from that point is a win.

Asking questions is a great way to learn and clarify your constraints and focus your intentions. And so is making mistakes. It is part of growth and progress to learn constantly.

It will not be easy to adhere to the constraints you discover. You might learn things about what you have done in the past that you wished you never knew. This could be discouraging. If you are convinced that the constraint your beliefs could put on your design practice are an inherent part of designing, it is a great opportunity to design a truly good solution.

Most people are comfortable in their ignorance of reality. But if you acquire knowledge and do not act on it, it is mentally much harder than just not asking the questions. Wanting to maintain a system that is rewarding for us, enabling us, and providing us with a vast supply of new desirable objects is very tempting. Unfortunately, it is also one of the main reasons the fashion industry has thrived on bad behaviour for so long – because nobody questioned its methods of work.

Modern times

One way of overcoming your discouragement is to realize the sheer power you hold. Remember that the fashion industry is only the sum of all the human parts. If one part malfunctions, it might be replaced. But if one part simply changes its ways of functioning, the system will change.

It can be overwhelming to face a monstrous system that absorbs everything in its way. In a gigantic maze, each player seems so small and even entirely lost.

The great thing about a machine is, that all its parts have a necessary role and function. If one part is altered, the machine and its functioning alter. If just one person changes their set of beliefs and changes their behaviour without leaving the fashion industry, it might start changing the whole industry. The more people rethink and alter their course, the faster it will start moving, until it accelerates into an unstoppable movement forward that will create new habits and traditions. And you will be part of it.

So, change your way of functioning!

Fashion likes to adopt the new. It is in active pursuit of the new. At its core, this is what it cares about the most. People working in this industry are trained to be on the lookout, to recognize the new next big thing before anybody else does.

Today, the call for sustainable fashion is presenting itself as the next big thing. It started to grow over 30 years ago, and it is still gaining momentum. Now, its call is omnipresent. People in the fashion industry respond like they have always done: they see it as a trend they need to fit into their practice.

But this time around, it is not something that can just be implemented in the current regular practice. It requires a new practice altogether.

We need to really change.

Our current time are often referred to as the Anthropocene[4] . This means we have entered an era where human activity has impacted the environment enough to constitute profound environmental changes. While nature and life on earth has been changing on its own for 4.5 billion years, humans are now the main influence, and we therefore have to take responsibility for the changes we are causing, whether they are intentional or not. The mere fact that we are driving change makes us liable.

Fashion is equal parts human inequality and contributing factor to climate change. Our habits, cultures and lifestyles perpetuate these destructive forces. This planet is our only home, and it deserves much better care.

Where do we start?

Ask questions!

In my company we do our due diligence about the materials we choose to use. We ask questions, we want to know all about the process with which the material is made. This also means that we are sometimes more hesitant than others when it comes to truly new materials. If we don't understand the process, or if the company does not want to disclose it, how can we judge if it fits with our values?

I love asking questions and learning more each day. However, I also believe in something like intuition. When something sounds fishy, it usually is. When it sounds too good to be true? Make sure you understand exactly how the miracle takes place.

---

4. The term is debatable, however. Anthropocene might create the illusion that the current ecological state of emergency is the result of humans being humans. In "The History of the World in 7 Cheap Things," Raj Patel and Jason W Moore propose the term Capitalocene, because they argue the reality today is that our emergency is the result of the specific historical phenomenon of capitalism.

When you feel that you need to ask more questions, do. It happens so often that brands or suppliers explain something, and I don't understand but I do not feel bad, or inadequate – I just keep asking until I fully understand what they mean. And everyone should learn to do the same.

This will be your most powerful tool. If you do not understand something, then good judgement is impossible. And if you keep having doubts, my motto is to stay away for the time being. I would rather avoid use and cause no harm, than to use ignorantly and potentially cause a lot of harm.

A key factor in developing a sustainable collection is to question. Do not assume someone else's values are aligned with yours, or even that their practices respect the planet. Do not assume they do things the best possible way.

The mere fact that you are reading this book means that you are aware that we work in an extremely polluting industry that has a lot of challenges.[5] Many things we take for granted could, and in my opinion should, be questioned. We need to have the courage to address these issues and formulate our answers to them.

Oblivion can be a wonderfully numbing state to be in; it makes you feel irresponsible, because you don't know any better. But you *are* responsible. As somebody working in the fashion industry, it is your job to know what happens behind the curtain. So, ask the farmer and the factory worker, ask the buyer and consumer, ask the seamstress and the dyer. Challenge how fashion is made and work towards re-connecting the broken links in your supply cycle. Encourage dialogue and exchange. It is your job to ask the questions and understand the processes that happen. You are co-responsible for them. And if you don't like them, then start redesigning them!

---

5. The main fashion challenges being; overconsumption, pollution on all levels, poor work compensation and an overall lack of transparency.

To be able to ask all the relevant questions, we first need to learn to see change as a positive challenge to our practice. As a designer you have a desire to create. To make and materialize a vision. The only way to integrate the challenging sustainability questions with a positive outlook, is if they are integrated in the vision.

Imagining your pieces being made

Let's challenge our vision. A brilliant concept for a collection should never include people in slavery working on it, unless it is a political statement to expose this misconduct. It would never include a desire to pollute and taint a river shocking pink, or hunter green, in some far away village, in some far away country.

When we integrate our social, ecological, political, anthropological dreams for society into our conceptual thinking we enter a new world. In this new reality, a designer creates their vision, defines their creative universe, intrinsic with the ethical position.

> "Everyone designs who devises courses of action aimed
> at changing existing situations into preferred ones.[6] "

For years, designers were not confronted with the consequences of their ideas. We trained designers not to think about the long-term consequences of their choices. We accepted that the impact far away from home was not investigated.[7] We live in a globalized society, yet we easily fail to see the impact we have on the other side of the globe.

Increasingly this is no longer accepted. Not by the consumers, not by the stakeholders, and not by the creators.

It demands that we take a position when we create. That we are informed about our product to an extent we have long forgotten. Hiding behind ignorance is no longer possible. Our world is overly informed, and we have all the tools to stay informed. We cannot

---

6. Herbert Simon, The sciences of the Artificial, (Cambridge: The MIT Press, 1969) Pg 111.

7. Dirty Laundry, Unravelling the corporate connections to toxic water pollution in China (Amsterdam: Greenpeace International, 2011)

accept that we don't know where or how our clothing is made, and of what materials.

———————

Some basic facts: the making of clothing implies that we use textiles, that we colour our textiles, and that many different hands work on the garments. Whether we look at garments from the viewpoint of a fast fashion retailer, or of a small independent designer, clothing, without exception, is made by people, not merely machines.

So, when we design clothing, we become co-responsible for the people that work on our clothing: for their health and wellbeing, for their working conditions and how they are treated, regardless of where on the globe the garments are produced.

And let's not forget what happens if we don't change. The result will be devastating to the planet and to humanity. And, because of the awareness you have today, it will be destructive for your mental health to continue acting like you did before.

Humans are changing life on this planet in a rapid and volatile way. Let's make sure it evolves and changes in ways we can be proud of. In ways for good. Remember that each of us has an impact. And it will require all of us.

Education in this is key: let learning and questioning become second nature. Protect your curious mind, investigate and innovate in sustainable ways.

Accept that others might not understand the urgency or necessity for this change. Being a fashion designer means advocating for something new all the time. Presenting things in ways nobody has seen them before. The sustainability challenge is no exception. Rise to the occasion and advocate for your values to be an engine for change.

Be proud to set out on this path of change.

Monitor how well you project your concerns to others. When you take a radical turn for the better, when you are designing the best possible objects positively impacting our planet and its inhabitants, let humanity see your achievements and share your inventions with them. Talk about what you do, teach the people around you, spread awareness and keep the momentum going.

Needles to say, it makes sense to keep making clothes. Not because we need them. There are enough clothes produced to dress the next three generations. But people are still consuming, buying, wearing different clothing. So it makes sense to offer them innovative, desirable and positive options to choose from. These clothes can make a difference, have a positive impact, and show our alliance with our planet.

Three

Transparency

FASHION IS TODAY DESIGNED, tried, and prototyped. A sales sample is made and then the product is shown to an audience. We still indicate if it is female, male, unisex. We also often divide it into seasons: a cruise collection, winter, summer, haute couture. Classifying what it is makes it easier to convince us of its necessity. And it creates a sense of urgency: it will be gone soon, so we need to purchase it now. It is also a necessity for the marketing and sales: one must be able to communicate to the right people, i.e., the store owners that sell your price range and whose clientele is your target audience. Your collection must be in shops when skiing season starts if you want to sell any high-endurance ski jackets. Showing and selling your collection to shops that only sell menswear would not be very efficient if you were designing women's bikinis after all, so classification is key from the start. Being able to say what it is and for whom. Those classifications do not support a more equal, just and open design by any means.

High-end fashion is presented during a fair, a fashion week, a multi-brand showroom. And after the sales period, where the idea is sold to designated boutiques and multi-brand stores, it is time to produce your invention.

The illusion of fashion engineering

In the fashion fairy-tale of making green products easily, the illusion goes something like this: when the sales sample is made, show on catwalks and sold, product engineers who are hired or are already on-staff will break down the design to analyse material choices, fabric treatments, embellishments, haberdashery.

This genius team will study all the components, judge the skills required to make the complete piece, and only then will the fashion technicians find the right green supplier of fabric to reproduce the idea, the craftsmen that can make the embellishments, an accessory supplier that develops the elements already chosen for sampling, but in a better, greener way.

And all these elements will replace the original piece that was sampled and shown to the clients and sold. This new version will look exactly like the old one, but it will be better: greener and more sustainable.

What a dream this would be for the designer, and what an enormous job for the beleaguered product engineer. Moreover, by no means would this count as a green practice. We don't first create a monstrous hybrid, made by undervalued, underpaid hands somewhere faraway, to then replace it by a cleaner production line. Not only is it impossible to simply remake it green, but it is also not how the garment was designed. The engineer might be able to fix a few of the worst problems, but the key decisions are embedded in the faulty design. True sustainable products need to be designed to have a positive impact from the start.

The absurdity of this illusion is clear, so why not do it right from the beginning?

The power of numbers and teamwork

It will require interdisciplinary teamwork to discuss, research, question and combine all the knowledge available to the team. And your team is much more well-informed, erudite, and proficient than you might think. By including both designers and engineers, all angles can be covered to make optimal positive decisions every step of the design and development process.

Working within such a sustainable holistic mindset, my biggest thrill is that of discovery. Each time a new material is launched, or an old and forgotten technique is resurfaces it sends a shiver of excitement down my spine. What can we do with it? How can it enrich our design language? What are its limits, and how far can we push them? Each designer longs for great materials with which to visualise the dream. As much as it excites you as a designer to discover something new with great potential, be cognisant that a textile engineer looking to make a change is waiting, searching, hoping to work for you.

Together real magic might happen.

Over the years I've gained a great deal of knowledge on how textiles are made. And the more I know, the more I realize that there is so much more to learn. Knowledge is power. Knowledge allows you to investigate the borders of what sustainability tomorrow can mean., or fashion for that matter.

If you strike up a conversation with a textile mill owner or weaver, they know the problems of dyeing, wet processing, curing of materials. And their knowledge is worth the world if the goal is to instigate change. As a designer, your sole purpose might feel like it is only about actualising the aesthetic dream but always remember that technicians hold the key to realizing those dreams and many more.

My team always tries to collaborate fully with our mills and textile weavers. While we experiment and discuss possible changes to the way things are done, we also listen closely to why the old way of doing things remains. What are technical requirements to accomplish change? In the end, the goal is to create sustainable change. This means it needs to be good for the planet on every level together with the potential of an everlasting life.

To create a material like that, technicians and chemists hold the key. If we imagine change, the difference needs to entail a status quo or improvement on every level. It should never be a better solution for one problem yet create a new, lesser problem. That would not uphold the tenet of true change.

It is in the synergy between designers – their visions and dreams – and technicians – that get inspired to realize those dreams – that positive change happens.

For a design to reach its full aesthetic potential, it needs to be surrounded by knowledge. As I've shown, it's absurd to make a product and in its final production stage decide to turn it sustainable – the sustainability question needs to be tackled first and foremost before and during the design phase.

Call it out

The fashion industry thrives in the shadows and celebrates obscurity. Obscurity, until now, was the main facilitator of all misconduct.

On 24 April 2013, the Rana Plaza building in Bangladesh collapsed. More than 1,100 people died and another 2,500 were injured making it the fourth largest industrial disaster in history. The victims were mostly young women. They were manufacturing clothing for well-known global fashion brands. It came as a shock to many consumers and fashion industry professionals alike.

Since then, an organization called *Fashion Revolution* has become a global movement calling for greater transparency, sustainability, and ethics in the fashion industry. The public demands sustainable business practice. Legislation is changing to force brands to use better practices but few talk about what these practices should look like. To be able to start envisioning new practices, knowledge is key. Without knowledge no informed choices are possible; with knowledge not choosing is no longer possible. Simply not acting upon one's knowledge is choosing a side in history: As the quotation often attributed to Edmund Burke goes: "The only thing necessary for evil to triumph in the world is that good men do nothing."[1]

---

1. https://en.wikipedia.org/wiki/Edmund_Burke#%22When_goo
d_men_do_nothing%22

If we want to maintain fashion as a beautiful artefact, we need to truly consider how our resources are deployed. Alongside that, the acceleration in climate change is something that most of us can not predict; all we know is that its implications will drastically impact the ways in which we are living. We are all creating a potentially perfect storm. Fashion's practices are part of that and yet, if only we would think differently, we could be part of a solution that rebalances the way in which we are living.

Trace your steps

Fashion is a global industry with an estimated worth of over $2.4 trillion dollars.[2] It employs around 50 million people[3] and is sometimes referred to as the second most polluting industry in the world right behind fossil fuels and oil.[4] Modern day slavery is an endemic part of fashion's business, and the lack of transparency and traceability across fashion supply chains are a major challenge. Fashion has the room and power to make positive change, and collaboration plays an important role in beginning to re-imagine the current, damaging systems.[5]

However absurd the idea, today, most garments developed around the globe are made by people unable to afford them. The way the

---

2. The global projected value for the fashion industry for 2016, was $2.4 trillion and only grew since then, even with the temporary set back during 2019 and 2020. Imram Amed Et Al., The State of Fashion 2017 (London,: McKinsey&Company & BOF, 2016)

3. As of 2017 it was estimated that 50 million people worked in the Fashion Industry. A sustainability report even suggest that the figure is 60 million people. Jonas Eder-Hansen Et Al., Pulse of the Fashion Industry 2017 (n.d.: Global Fashion Agenda & The Boston Consulting Group, 2017)

4. This is a very debatable claim, many researchers do not accept this statement, neither do it. The origin of the claim is rather obscure and there is no information about how that idea was calculated.

5. Fashion Revolution has teamed up with Future learn, giving great courses on how to become an activist for change. On a permanent basis the Fashion Revolution organization calls upon global citizens to take action to right the wrongs of the industry. They are an active beacon of information and work in decentralized volunteer lead groups all over the globe inspiring and demanding much needed change.

system operates relies on boarders: boarders between rich and poor.[6] Garments are made to cater to an audience with a limitless desire for cheap new things. And they are made by people with little or no influence on its price. In many factories around the world the idea of a union is feared. Empowering workers and giving them a say in the things they make, the prices charged, or how they make them will cause customers fleeing from them. To produce cheap clothing, cheap labour is essential.

This is how the fashion industry leaches the poorest in the world to supply cheap work. When factory workers become demanding or get a salary increase, the factory is swapped for another. The business model relies on exploitation, pushing the purchase price down to the unbearable minimum to make the maximum amount of profit on the sales. The most tragic part of this story is that the labour costs of any garment are a fraction of its total cost and raising the wages of the makers to a living wage[7], would only have around a 5% increase on the price of the final garment.[8]

---

6. For an excellent read on how the world as we know it is shaped by cheap things; Raj Patel & Jason W Moore, History of the Wold in Seven Cheap Things: A Guide to Capitalism, Nature and the Future of the Planet. One of the main thoughts in the book is that Capitalism not only has frontiers; it exists only through frontiers.

7. Living wage is a wage a worker earns in a standard working week that is enough to provide them and their family's basic needs, including food, housing, clothing, education, and healthcare. Minimum wage is the lowest wage rate set by the government at which companies are legally required to pay workers, in developing countries this is often set at the UN poverty level, which is US € 1.90 / day.

8. Anne Lally, Climbing the Ladder to Living Wages, An Update on FWF's Living Wage research 2011 – 2022 (Amsterdam: Fair Wear Foundation, 2012) pg 16 – 21

TIER 4
Raw material extraction / processing

Farm   Feedstock   Recycling   Fibre producer

TIER 3
Raw material processing

Ginning   Spining & carding

TIER 2
Production of all components and processes

Knitting   Weaving   Dyeing & printing   Finishing   Trims

TIER 1
Product manufacturing

Cutting   Sewing   Finishing   Washing & dyeing

TIER 0

Stores   Offices   Design studio   Agent, warehouse & repacking

Logistics: shipping of materials and products across to world to the next step in the value chain

Consumer care:
washing,
drying,
dry cleaning,
repair, etc.

End of life:
reuse,
recycle,
landfill.

Healthcare, benefits, fair wages are a distant siren call for most people making anything we wear. Exploitation, sexual harassment and living insecurity are a daily reality. To really understand how inconsequential the price increase would be, all you need to be aware of is that a T-shirt priced €29,00 at retail would only become € 30,57.

Solid partnerships

Brands operating in the textile industry claim that consumers are unwilling to accept price increases to pay living wages. In a way this is true: about 75% of apparel purchases are now made at discounted prices.[9] But a study by Censuswide in 2014 found that 52% of shop-

---

9. Informally we have heard on several occasions that about 70% of garments sold, sell at reduced prices during flash discounts, seasonal promotions etc. online. A 60% return rate is considered industry standard for online sales.

pers would be willing to pay higher prices if they had the reassurance that workers were paid a living wage. Consumers would be prepared to pay 15% on a $100 garment and 28% more on a $10 item with the guarantee that the piece was made in good working conditions.[10] It therefore begs the question whether companies value their profit over poor people's living conditions? Time has shown that if a country takes action, increases the minimum wage, or makes any other regulation beneficial to worker living standards, brands start looking for a new, cheaper country.

Besides this constant quest for cheaper labour, the world witnessed a prime example of how unconcerned brands are with worker well-being during the global Covid-19 pandemic. Big, global companies refused to pay for work already finished, because they no longer wanted to receive the goods. Boxes were left standing ready in ports with nobody willing to ship them to the stores or pay for work already completed. On top of that, factories in Bangladesh, the Philippines and India reported a cancellation of 90% of their orders already in processing. You might reason that each company is protecting its bottom line and should react when this is threatened, but if you rely on exploiting people working in countries with no healthcare, social insurance, or possibility to create any savings, don't you have a responsibility towards them when times are tough?

---

10. Robert Pollin, Justine Burns and James Heintz, Global apparel production and sweatshop labour: can raising retail prices finance living wages? In Cambridge Journal of Economics, Vol. 28, No. 2 (Oxford: Oxford University Press, 2004) pg. 153 – 171

Be transparent about money

Production Cost

Yellow Waffle Dress with Embroidery

Product Code: S17 105B
Product Description: Yellow Waffle Dress with Embroidery
Manufacturer: Pereira & Rocha Lda, Portugal

RETAIL MARKUP: 74,82€

TOTAL COST, NET: 124,70€

VAT 19%: 23,70€

TOTAL COST INCL. 19% VAT: 148,40€

MATERIAL COST: 10,61€
Fabric: 0,84m / 8,90€
Bias tape: 0,22m / 1,38€
Button: 1 pc / 0,33€

DEVELOPING COST: 1,63€
Sample: 0,37€
Pattern: 0,62€
Digitizing: 0,64€

MANUFACTURING COST: 12,40€
Sewing + embroidery at Pereira & Rocha, Lda, Portugal

PACKAGING COST: 0,30€
Size + brand label: 1 pc / 0,05€
Care label: 1 pc / 0,05€
Hangtag: 1 pc / 0,20€

WHOLESALE MARKUP: 24,94€
Logistics for production: 3,43€
Photography + content production: 0,65€
Administrative + bookkeeping: 4,11€
Marketing: 5,75€
Margin: 11€

By making clothing so inexpensive with no respect for fair pricing at almost all levels of the supply chain, society now believes garments are a cheap commodity.

Transparency is the first step

One way of levelling the playing field is by creating transparency. Transparency means that a company knows who made their clothes and textiles, where they are made and under what conditions, and they share this information with the public.

It might seem like the first part of the definition is evident, but in today's world, certain fashion companies never even visit the factories that make their clothes. They have no idea about the conditions or the faces behind the emails. Suppliers face impossibly tight deadlines, which might give them no option other than to outsource, because it makes economic sense, to another company that can perform the task cheaper/faster.

My point is this: many companies have no idea who or how their clothes are made, and those who think they know, might, under further inspection find that their orders are outsourced to cheaper workers elsewhere without their knowledge.

Be transparent about suppliers & certificates

Material Information

Yellow Waffle Dress with Embroidery

Product Code: S17 105B
Product Description: Yellow Waffle Dress with Embroidery
Manufacturer: Pereira & Rocha Lda, Portugal

COTTON THREAD
100% organic cotton
GOTS certified
Supplier: MANIFATTURA ITALIANA CUCIRINI spa –
MIC spa, Italy

EMBROIDERY THREAD
100% organic cotton
GOTS certified
Supplier: MANIFATTURA ITALIANA CUCIRINI spa –
MIC spa, Italy

FABRIC
Main Fabric: VANILLE WAFFLE HONEYCOMB
Composition: 100% certified organic cotton,
GOTS certified
Weight: 280g/m²
Supplier: Gebr. Elmer & Zweifel GmbH & Co. KG,
Germany

SIZE + BRAND LABEL
Berliner Textil Etiketten GmbH, Germany
Composition: 100% recycled polyester

BIAS TAPE
Main Fabric: WHITE POPLIN
Composition: 100% certified organic cotton
Supplier: Ecological Textiles, The Netherlands

CARE LABEL
Pereira & Rocha Lda, Portugal
Composition: 100% organic cotton

BUTTON
100% coconut shell
Supplier: Knopf und Knopf International GmbH & Co. KG,
Germany

HANGTAG
Cardboard, FSC certified
Supplier: SUPER EXCELLENT INDUSTRY CO.,LIMITED,
China

Each of us must find their way to deal with the fashion industry's inherent tendency and long ingrained habits to hide and devalue individual contribution to uphold the dream of limitless beauty. Being transparent about your actions is a great start: it makes you accountable and creates the opportunity to improve.

In this light, the concept of company trade secrets is very problematic. Historically it has proven a useful key to competitive success but secrets, by definition, obscure information. History has shown us time and again that generally, this veil of secrecy is not used for good, but rather for evil. So how do we deal with this? What would happen if you opened up the system? If all marketing and communication includes information about your actions? Where, how, and for how much did you make this item? The Honest By website developed by Bruno Pieters was a beautiful example of transparency in action. Not only did they pioneer listing all their suppliers, but it also included how much money of your garment went to each part of the value chain. Scrolling through the website, helped you to comprehend the price of the garment, and thus its value rose instantly.

Brands should know in exactly which factory their products are sewn, how much the garment worker who made it was paid, and even the name and position of that person. Expand your idea of team. Include the workers, rely on their knowledge, and improve their lives. Then the brand will automatically know in which country the garment was made, and more.

But why stop here? A brand should also know where and how the fibre was grown, harvested, or extracted. What chemicals and toxins were used to achieve the desired dye and finishing on the material? If today brands do not know this, how can they optimize the design? Maybe a different design would have a more positive general footprint; because only if you know the type of finishing used, and its alternatives on the market, can you ask to exchange it for an environmentally friendlier one.

To determine how positive a garment is, a brand needs to know how much energy is consumed to make the garment, how much water is used by the full supply cycle, and what the carbon emission is for the entire development of the garment.

All this information together reveals the true nature of the garment. Does it have a positive impact? Where is it failing? And what kind of end of life or recycle plan is embedded in the design of the garment? Does the consumer know to let the garment reach its full potential positive impact? Only when you know and have data on each step, can you make proper improvements to the design.

Four

Life cycles, nutrients, and Cradle to Cradle® thinking

Footprints and Snail trails

DURING THE EXHIBITION "A Poem That Is Not Our Own" I had the pleasure of hearing William Kentridge talk about his thought processes while making his films and art works. He referred to his practice of drawing and erasing and his initial desire to hide all traces of erasing. And he explained how he failed. In his own words:

> "It took quite a while for me to understand that the visible snail's trail of every object in the drawing was in fact part of their virtue. And did become in fact part of the meaning, whether I liked it or not, that the films became about the persistence of memory, or the process of time being made visible."[1]

Just like Kentridge, we too will benefit from realising we leave footsteps behind us that are impossible to erase. When we make something, why not accept that it is meant to leave a trail?

The beauty of nature is that every living part of it leaves "a snail trail" that is needed for all other life. Snails mechanically modify the physical structure of the soil as they leave their trail, as do earthworms

---

1. William Kentridge, Artist talk, during Art Basel, Basel, June 18, 2019.

as they crawl through the earth. Both digest organic matter mould that they pull from soil litter. Through these activities they transport nutrients into the mineral layers of soil. The discarded waste, or snail trail, leaves undigested materials where bacteria and other decomposers gain access to the nutrients. Bodies of dead worms passively add mineral nutrients to the soil. By their mere existence these creatures participate in the production of the ecosystem and create a feedback loop in a much bigger recycling process.[2] This process of nutrient cycling has a historical foothold in the writings of Charles Darwin in reference to the decomposition actions of earthworms. Darwin described it as "the continued movement of the particles of earth".[3]

Somewhere along the way, humankind has stopped the continued movement of particles by introducing the idea of waste. Waste has no value, and we discard it in ways that do nothing for our earth, through landfills and incineration. Nature does not know the concept of waste: everything is interconnected in cycles of nurture.

The underlying idea of Cradle to Cradle®[4] is that, for sustainable business strategy, it is best practice to mimic the regenerative cycle of nature in which waste is reused endlessly. In nature, when any living organism dies or creates waste, that waste breaks down and becomes nutrients for another process.

2. Sébastien Barot, Alexis Ugolini, Fadia Bekkal Brikci, Nutrient cycling efficiency explains the long-term effect of ecosystem engineers on primary production. In Functional Ecology Vol 21 (2007) pg. 1-10

3. Charles Darwin, The Formation of Vegetable Mould, through the Action of Worms, with Observation on their habits. (London: John Murray, 1881) pg. 230

4. Cradle to Cradle® is a registered trademark of MBDC McDonough Braungart Design Chemistry. undefinedCradle to Cradle CertifiedTM is a certification mark licensed by the Cradle to Cradle Products Innovation Institute.

This idea implies no longer addressing waste as a problem, or something to discard, but rather as an eternal resource for future use. In both Dutch and German waste is also called *afval (Abfall)*, literally translated as "that which falls off". This can be regarded as food or the base for something else for which we can create a purpose, and we should thus recognise its inherent value instead of simply relegating it to trash.

Let's examine the tree cycle that is described by the founders of Cradle to Cradle® (C2C). It illustrates a design thinking that holds many keys for fashion to improve how it functions.

A tree lives and grows. If left uninterrupted, it creates the opportunity for animals to call it home. During life it: actively transforms CO_2; feeds the surrounding soil with nutrients; creates shade and cools surroundings; bears fruit and the potential for new trees. If after a long life, it is cut and morphs into a table using only toxin-free glue or a simple dovetail joint then this means the tree-now-table is still a fully natural object, fully recyclable. It can host many dinners, and can be passed down from generation to generation, becoming an heirloom, treasured and loved. When it is no longer used, or out of fashion, it might be transformed into a new life cycle: it might become cooking spoons, coasters, earrings, and serve yet another long life in its third cycle form.

Centuries after its first life started, it can re-enter a transformation stage and become yet again something new like paper. If during all its lives only nontoxic glues, biological inks and paints are used, it is still fully compostable. After it has been read and is no longer needed, the paper can be discarded, and transformed into hummus, feeding many insects and enriching the soil so new trees will grow abundantly. Over the length of many centuries, this tree can have several incarnation, and none of them will disturb or threaten its future, so that no cycle destroys the nutrients that are the essence of the tree.

In such a manner, at the end of its many lives, the tree can revert to becoming a soil nutrient.[5]

Thillustration exhibits how the goal is to not create just one cycle, but to design keeping in mind that, the piece you have made, will still hold the promise to become many more forms later, constantly creating new cycle after new cycle. And each cycle is respectful of the inherent nutrients the piece holds. What is vital for these multiple life cycles is, that throughout their multiple lives, nothing is introduced that could interrupt their biological system.

Left to its own devices, life always upcycles. There is no waste.

Two streams

The lifecycle idea is only viable for things that function within a biological system.

In fashion we love blending nutrients: fabric composed of cotton and polyester is common, while jersey with a percentage of stretch is preferred due to its comfort when worn. This needs to be examined with great caution as it mostly kills the potential future life of the material. When you take a biological nutrient and mix it with any kind of technical one you create a hybrid with no future life.

If the tree-as-table had been treated with toxic paints, or with epoxy varnish, the tree would have been robbed of its potential next life. Its capacity to re-morph again and again into something new would have been interrupted and it would become a waste product. It would no longer be possible to end it's cycle as food for new life.

---

5. William McDonough & Michael Braungart, The Upcycle: Beyond Sustainability – Designing for Abundance (New York: North Point Press, 2013) pg. 31-42

CRADLE TO CRADLE
After a concept by Michael Braungart and William McDonough

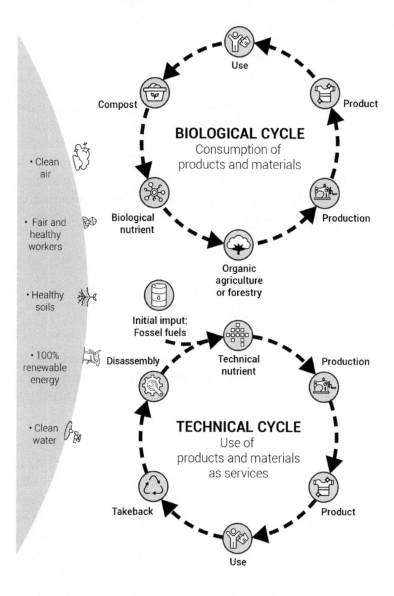

If we tried to compost it, it would leak heavy chemicals into the soil, poisoning everything around it, instead of nurturing and feeding it.

Biological systems grow and are endlessly giving life. This is nature's recycling system. Our actions should safeguard this feedback loop that uses and creates energy in the process of putting material resources back into use by decomposition. We can only nourish eternal regenerating, not by designing for eternity, but by maintaining the possibility of decomposition and growth.

Technical cycles are another story. Technical nutrients, where most polyesters belong, are not life-giving. They are inorganic or synthetic materials manufactured by humans, like plastics. Technical nutrients have great advantage: they can be used many times over with minimal loss of quality. Therefore, we must maintain these nutrients, because even though they don't transform into new forms like biological nutrients, we can recover them time and again to reuse endlessly, thus creating a technical cycle.

Technical nutrients must be reused.

Products need to be designed well so that they remain a nutrient in the biosphere or remain in the technosphere, and never contaminate the entire ecosystem. Only in this way, can they remain part of the ecosystem.

Considering all elements we use, as nutrients for a next phase, is one way to avoid waste for eternity. This seems self-evident for biological systems but I would go further and say that I believe it is vital for *both* systems. As technical systems contain metals that are non-replenishable yet are used like never before to make cell phones and other electronics, we dispose of them without any recuperation of the nutrients. They are lost for eternity if they end up in landfill. Technical systems are mostly created of fossil fuels. It seems unimaginable, but this too, we will run out of if we don't care more for what we have.

We need to replace our linear use of fossil fuels and non-renewable resources with an endless cycle of uncontaminated technical nutrients.

The challenge today is that most things around us are hybrids, using elements from the biological cycle and the technical cycle together with no masterplan of how to separate them back into their proper lifecycles later. Once a hybrid is made, and there is no design thought put into how to continue the lives of its biological and technical elements, we are creating garbage monsters. The cycles end and we have created waste. Facing the alternative of endless regeneration, this is very bad practice.

We are depleting the planet's resources and depriving potential future objects of their existence.

Today we live in a time of mass production. Most production is made with no closed-loop or final game plan. Our consumer products end up in the ocean, in Africa and Southeast Asia, in landfill, destroying economies, marine life, our waterways, our land, and our air. Our waste is making this planet inhabitable.[6]

We consume limitlessly, with little regard for how or of what things are made. The number of resources we annually consume requires about 1.7 planets to provide them. And we do not have 1.7 planets.

Our design challenge is to use Cradle to Cradle principles to design with no end in mind, creating products that can be reclaimed using materials that can be recycled or reused — then, and only then, can we provide accessible, easy ways for consumers to return products

---

6. An estimated 70% of all clothing donated to 2nd hand globally end up in Africa, destroying the local market and polluting the local ecosystem. An estimated 80% of people in Kenya and Uganda wears 2nd hand clothing imported from wealthy nations. Foreign correspondent, Dead White Man's Clothes producer Alison McClymont (ABC News, 2021) based on the immersive multimedia research project: Dead White Man's Clothes. Executive director Liz Ricketts (2016 – Present)

into the reuse cycle once those products are no longer needed. Only if everyone participates, can we make sure that all nutrients around us are never lost and can continue their natural endless lifecycles.

Circular design is a strategy that aims to use the planet's finite resources in a sustainable way. In circular design any material is considered to be part of a loop or a system, where recovery for future use is anticipated and enabled. The aim is to keep materials in circulation in perpetuity.

Product categories

All products that exist today can be divided into three categories: products of consumption, products of service, and product that should not be on the market.

Products of consumption, such as cleaning chemicals, plant-based clothing, shampoos, and packaging materials, are made from biological nutrients and should be designed for safe disposal in the natural environment. This means avoiding coating cotton fibres with silicone to create the non-iron shirt as it makes it a hybrid with no way of returning to a nutrient for something else.

Products of service, such as cars, washing machines, most polyester clothing and televisions, are made from technical nutrients and designed to provide a service to users and then to be recycled.

Product that should not be on the market such as hazardous waste and hybrids of both nutrients are a big problem. Today they are very marketable (consumers love them) yet totally unsustainable. These products contain X-rated chemicals are directly and actively destroying human and planetary health. Hybrids will after use become useless waste. We should get rid of those as soon as possible, as they are not fit to be used in an environmentally-sound way, and should be discontinued and substituted as immediately.[7]

If this thinking is truly adopted, it becomes very clear and simple to identify your product category, choose your materials and your making strategies.

Supply needs together

We can use design as a sign of intention. By stating your values, intention, and ambitions loud and clear, you send out a signal to consumers and other companies. It might inspire competitor companies to up their game. It might inspire supplier companies to redirect their research and product line. That one signal can create a ripple effect.

This might also inspire and motivate other companies to direct their energies into realising or solving a partial problem you are encountering. Nobody can achieve all necessary positive progress on their own, but we can rely on our network for support.

It is also smart business to state your intent and the problems you encounter. If you are struggling, so are others. It means there is a business opportunity, there is a demand and thus a market. By focussing attention on what is needed, more minds will be addressing the issues you encounter, and so the bigger the likelihood of a solution surfacing.

By creating demand, textile suppliers and other suppliers will try to create to supply your needs.

At Infantium Victoria, we stated our values and ethics unequivocally from the beginning. We favoured suppliers that worked in the same or similar value framework as ours. But we did more than that. We reached out to companies with knowledge and expertise, and an

---

7. For much more insight and information, Michael Braungart, William McDonough, EPEA Internationale Umweltforschung GmbH, and McDonough Braungart Design Chemistry LLC.

open mind to implement change. We asked them for support and helped them change with us.

One of our favourite collaboration partners since the beginning has been a family-owned weaver in Portugal. They have been working for over 90 years and hold a treasure trove of expertise in making woollen jacquard fabrics. At one fabric fair, we initiated a conversation, asking about how they developed new ideas, and what their vision was for the future. We discovered we had a lot of shared values. As part of their product range, they had made four different fabrics in organic cotton, to see how the market would respond. Each fabric was rather plain and simple, an easy starting point. Our first season together we used their products to investigate quality, and establish a working relationship. From season two we became bolder, asking to transform some of their jacquard fabrics into organic cotton. They were and are a wool textile specialist, but we are a vegan company. By not judging or dismissing them at the start but looking for common ground and exchange we now are in our eighth year of collaboration, and we have created countless unique made-to-measure jacquards with them that have become cornerstones of our collections and eye-catchers for the public.

Other problems we have encountered early on have not yet been solved, and are still a thorn in my side. One example is our search for heavy duty packaging solutions for rolls of fabric. Ever since our first season, we have received beautiful, unpolluted plant-based materials from suppliers in heavy duty plastic. Since I want to keep my office as plastic-free as I can, we always reuse the plastic to rewrap the rolls for shipment to our factories. But I would love to have an alternative. It was a relief to realise that big companies like Filippa Ka are struggling with the same problem. This means a lot more people are working on a solution.

We have been looking into biologically compostable plastics, but none of them have the necessary heavy duty qualities. Since we recently expanded our business into made in India fabrics that are exported to Europe, the problem has now a new sense of urgency.

But we still haven't found a *good* positive solution. For now, we are employing the old local technique of sewing fabric in jute for transport, and we add a layer of thin biodegradable plastic underneath it, for any potential water damage, and a layer of paper to act as barrier in case anything happens to the biodegradable plastic, so that the fabric is not in direct contact with it.

Clearly this is not an ideal solution, but it's the best we have come across so far.

Since we are very aware of the problem, I raise the question at forums, during informal exchanges with big brands, and am constantly on the lookout for a breakthrough solution. It is great to learn that much bigger companies are struggling with the same, and it means that if a solution hits the market, there will instantly be an economically viable direct customer base for it.

Research has determined that snails appear to gain energetic benefits when following in the tracks of another, and more recent trails confer greater benefits.[8] If we understand this, we will see that there is no need for each company to invent all solutions. With transparency we can share our discoveries and knowledge to move faster and with more energy into a positive future.

Part of ensuring that you understand the cycle of nutrients you are working with, is thoroughly knowing the composition of all your ingredients and sub ingredients.

This can be a long and tedious process requiring a lot of chemistry and technical understanding. It includes all dyes, fasteners, plastics, metals, finishes, and auxiliaries. The logical first steps at the beginning of any C2C thinking is stating your values, and charting

8. Gary B. Gillis, Snail Trails. In Journal of Experimental Biology, Vol 210, Issue 17 (Sept. 2017) 10.1242

your nutrients. This means investigating and asking your suppliers about the exact composition of each element you use, and moving down the supply chain, step by step, to identify each treatment and intervention that happens along the chain.

When you start designing something, first choose and reflect what system your product will fit into. Define its journey there and then.

Know before doing anything if you need your product to be in a biological cycle or a technical cycle.

The UN estimates that 80% of the impact of a product is decided at the design stage. This places a big responsibility on the shoulders of any designer.

If the design job is done well, the consumer can be relieved of so many hard questions. If the garment has a clear after-life path, it is clear how to dispose of it, and how it will re-enter the natural resource loop. If the garment decomposes without pollution, it can be recycled to a new and high-quality product, and customers will no longer feel any guilt for the consumption habits. Their problems will have been solved long before they desired the object.

The designer has such a decisive voice. It is the birthplace of each new product. If we change its birth form, we change its life.

The root of the problem is also the root of the solution hence the root needs to have a good starting place.

GLOBAL FIBRE BASKET 2021

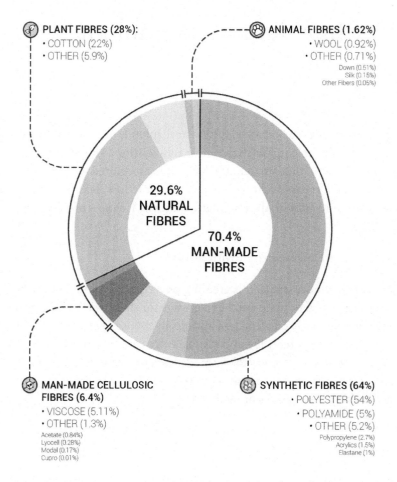

PLANT FIBRES (28%):
• COTTON (22%)
• OTHER (5.9%)

ANIMAL FIBRES (1.62%)
• WOOL (0.92%)
• OTHER (0.71%)
Down (0.51%)
Silk (0.15%)
Other Fibers (0.05%)

29.6%
NATURAL
FIBRES

70.4%
MAN-MADE
FIBRES

MAN-MADE CELLULOSIC
FIBRES (6.4%)
• VISCOSE (5.11%)
• OTHER (1.3%)
Acetate (0.84%)
Lyocell (0.28%)
Modal (0.17%)
Cupro (0.01%)

SYNTHETIC FIBRES (64%)
• POLYESTER (54%)
• POLYAMIDE (5%)
• OTHER (5.2%)
Polypropylene (2.7%)
Acrylics (1.5%)
Elastane (1%)

Source: Textile Exchange, Preferred Fiber Materials Market Report 2022

Five

Rhythm: nature's pendulum

F ASHION LOVES ABUNDANCE! EXCESS and splendour are driving engines in its constant stream of reinvention. The paradox we currently live is that sustainable fashion is associated with poverty, less options to choose from, less enticing practices, less freedom to create in contrast with the abundant, limitless, richness of traditional fashion.

But is this premise coherent with reality?

The fashion industry itself is creating poverty on a massive scale by not paying society's poorest a living wage for their work. The industry is permanently creating less options to choose from by depleting our natural resources. It happens far away from us, and is hard to imagine, but almost every fabric made from polyester is another volume of fossil fuel that can never be recovered for any other purpose like making solar panels or medicine.

The freedom that designers talk ecstatically about, implies non accountability, and the blind use of the natural resources around us.

By using our natural resources as disposables, disrespecting the elements around us, we create a constant state of scarcity. What we use is only useful right now, in this state, and will disappear. Fashion today is comparable to a single-use plastic bag. Actually, it's even worse: both the fast fashion garment and the plastic bag are super cheap, and only used once or twice and then thrown away. Both end up in landfills, or drift into the oceans. But the single use plastic bag is relatively easy to recycle since it's made from a mono material.

Complex blends of materials making up a single fast fashion item makes it much harder – and mostly even impossible – to recycle.

The fashion industry is using nutrients that after a single use are taken out of service. They are no longer available for future use.[1] Any raw material that is transformed into an object, with only attention of its direct, first use, eliminates all other applications of that same raw material for the future.

Single use really means single use and never again. Thus, each design becomes just another step in the further depletion of our world. This is no place for fashion to thrive. This is not abundance. It is poverty and decay.

It can be the opposite. If we adapt our system to a positive, contributing system, where all is part of a participating circle, then fashion could blossom into something beyond what is imaginable today.

Safely generated abundance, created intentionally, can replace our current situation.[2] Maybe we will look back one day at this time in history and realize we are currently living in an oblivion of abundance, not noticing the scarcity and limitations that we are amplifying every day.

Yet, if we could just pause and look around, we will see that our earth creates in abundance. Regardless of what humans do, nature

---

1. Besides the fact that most garments are hard or impossible to recycle because of their blend of materials, fast fashion has convinced us that there is no need to reuse, repair or re-wear our clothing. Statistically, it is estimated that most clothing is worn actively only for 6 months, and estimates imply that about 30% of clothing is disposed before being sold, and about 10% is sold and never worn.

2. Paraphrased from William McDonough & Michael Braungart, The Upcycle: Beyond Sustainability – Designing for Abundance pg. 36

will bloom in spring, flourish in summer, bear fruits in autumn and become dormant in winter as a prelude of a new cycle starting again.

Humans have not been able to stop nature of doing this. But we do make it harder for her with our heedless, reckless intervention. Lucky for us, she has proven resilient.

When thinking about abundance, imagine how nature could flourish if we were more supportive, or if we only stopped actively sabotaging her.[3]

If we operate under the premiss of mutual respect, and don't deplete nature, yet instead nurture her, she will create more and more, in return providing for us. Nature's natural rhythm works in endless cycles of growth and regeneration.

The impact of fashion is something hard to track. Lack of transparency in the supply chain and the sheer size of the industry make it hard to comprehend exactly how impactful fashion is. Closely intertwined with the global primary polluting industry (the oil and gas industry),

---

3. In our endless efforts to control nature, we use carcinogenic chemicals to kill off plants we don't want. As a side effect bees are killed at a rapid rate, making natural procreation so much harder. The list of things we have damaged and are damaging in nature is too long. Some of these things are done on a national, industrial, or corporate level. But look around you, and question what you can do to support nature. By changing your behaviour, turning your garden to a bee heaven, by limiting your waste, and focusing on recycling, by stimulating your local government and local initiatives – so much small change can take place and it is all within your reach.

fashion depends heavily on it: oil and gas are what make their machines run and provide over 60% of the raw materials fashion uses.[4]

It is a fact that the fashion industry depletes natural resources, releases toxic chemicals, adds to greenhouse emissions, and creates millions of tonnes of waste.

Our planet's rhythm of life

If we want to really address the current situation: "We need to reinvent our eating and drinking, our moving and working, in our local ecosystems and local cultures. Enriching our lives by lowering our consumption, without impoverishing others. And above all, we need to subject the laws that govern production and consumption to the laws of Gaia; the laws of the planet."[5]

---

4. Since the 1950's the use of polyester has risen sharply, and today it accounts for a huge 60% of all textiles produced and used around the globe. Polyester, a polymer, is a by-product of the oil refinery process. The polymer most commonly used is Polyethylene Terephthalate (PET), a plastic derived from crude oil that's also used to make plastic bottles.

5. Dr. Vandana Shiva, Earth Democracy: Justice, Sustainability, and Peace. (Berkeley: North Atlantic Books, 2015)

In other words, aligning our human needs within planetary boundaries[6] is the basis of creating a sustainable society. And this thus not per se imply scarcity or making less. What it does mean is that we need to re-evaluate how we make everything, and how we think about the entirety of our society.

Contemplating the laws of the planet might seem rather vague, but it basically refers to what and how much of everything our planet provides; for example, we cannot use more water than there is on this planet; the planet is a defined volume of space that we are using and cultivating, living in, and depending on.

If we streamline how we treat our planet, it has the capacity to provide more than enough for all of us living today, it technically already does, her yields are just very unevenly distributed. And with the pro-

---

6. Planetary boundaries are a concept defined by Johan Rockström and Will Steffen and their team in 2009. It discusses earth processes that contain environmental boundaries. The goal of the team was to define a "safe operating space for humanity", something the international community including scientists, governments and any private or public organization could use to define sustainable development. According to their paradigm, "transgressing one or more planetary boundaries may be deleterious or even catastrophic due to the risk of crossing thresholds that will trigger non-linear, abrupt environmental change within continental- to planetary-scale systems." The planetary boundaries are divided into 10 categories, each with an indication of how much we can use to stay within safe planetary boundaries. In at least 3 of the 10 categories – biodiversity loss, nitrogen cycle and climate crisis – we have far exceeded any safe use of resources and safe limits. In other categories, we just don't have enough studies to know if we passed safe boundaries. Examples are: the levels of chemical pollution, and how the planet can recover from them, or the level of particle pollution of the atmosphere and how this evolves over time. undefinedJohan Rockström et al., Planetary Boundaries: Exploring the Safe Operating Space for Humanity. In, Ecology & Society, Vol. 14, No 2, Art 32 (2019) undefined

jected growth in population, it is all our best interest to better align our needs with earth's yields.

Good practice, in line with nature, means respecting nature's needs and limits. Working with her, rather than in disregard of her. Not just imposing any idea but observing what would be most beneficial in this specific circumstance. Questioning if certain progress we make is actual progress for all, or only short-term solutions and fixes for here and now.

If we respect nature's rhythm, we must adhere to her cycle and adapt to her scale.

When carbon dioxide is produced, we need to compare the levels we produce with the amounts that local trees can absorb. If this is not balanced, we must either produce less carbon, or plant more trees.

When crops are attributed to plots of land, we need to assess if groundwater levels are sufficient to provide them with what they need, to ensure that we do not need to extract water from elsewhere, and thereby potentially disturb or deplete whole lakes.[7] Local crops are adapted to local climates, so they will flourish easier, with less human intervention. Therefore, we must avoid monocultures in favour of multi-crop fields that rotate because while they are harder to harvest, the crops take care of each other, like siblings. One plant might distract another plant's pests thus keeping it safe; or the root system of one flora will enable the other vegetation to take grip and flourish as well.

---

7. The Aral Lake has evaporated due to the intense cotton growth that required extensive water extraction. In the beginning of the 20th century, this lake spanned 450 km north–south and 290 km east-west, was 69 metres deep, and was one of the eighth biggest lakes in the world. Today, it has almost entirely disappeared making it one of the biggest environmental dramas of our times. What makes matters worse, is that governments knew this would happen, but regarded the economic impact of cotton more important than the lake.

THE 9 PLANETARY BOUNDARIES

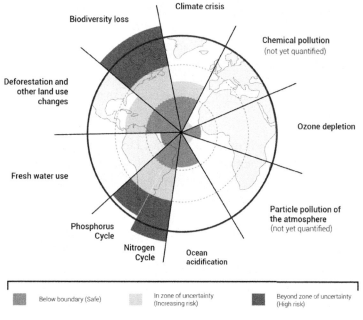

After Johan Rockström, Stockholm Resilience Centre et al. 2009

If you cultivate your plants with the desire that they grow strong and will have a positive long-term impact on the soil, do not over-water, don't use chemical fertilizers and pesticides that will weaken the plant in the long run. Choose the right plants for your environment, and surroundings that will be nurture it. By doing all that, the plant becomes sturdier, with stronger, deeper roots, more capable of reaching groundwater and drinking less[8].

---

8. Fukuoka decided not to flood his rice field, contrary to popular practice. Masanobu Fukuoka, The One-Straw Revolution, An Introduction to Natural Farming. (Emmaus: Rodale Press, 1978) pg. 15

When I visited a cotton farmer in the south of India, the field was growing regenerative organic cotton, next to a conventional field of cotton.[9] The visual difference could have not been more distinct. The conventional field was lush, with green leaves, high stocks, gently waving in the wind. Compared to this elegant sight, the stubby, brown, parched organic cotton plants looked like a bunch of dried out prickly bushes. Not a green leaf in sight, at least 30% shorter and not waving in the wind at all.

I later learned that while not a pretty sight, the organic plant does not require all this water to make useless green leaves, and it focusses all its energy in growing deep roots, capable of finding ground water. This root system is also what prevents desertification of the ground. Water and oxygen are retained in the soil, making it a nutrient rich environment.

9. The Reset Cotton team is doing a great job changing big parts of Indian agricultural land into regenerative farmland.

The field I visited belonged to a small family farm whose farmer, two years prior to my visit, began to transform his fields regeneratively and organically, in the hopes of improving his family's health. Allergies, breathing difficulties, persistent skin problems had formerly been a part of their lives. With the changes he implemented on his fields, he had already noticed a drastic improvement in his family's health, and enjoyed watching his fields bloom with local seeds, not needing the expensive chemical treatments he had previously become accustomed to using.

It was a process, for the farmer to understand that after the harvest season it was not in his best interest to burn the cotton stems, but to find other ways of using them to profit him and his field. He was now able to compost part of it, while transforming another part into the ground element for floorboards. It has long been common practice in many parts of the world to burn whatever is left in the fields after harvest – and it is such a waste! All those nutrients lost instead of being returned to the soil in different ways, the most common of course being composting the vegetation.

Nature does not produce waste. Whatever a field generates that we do not utilize, we need to figure out how it can continue its natural cycle of reinventing itself, as it is not waste.

Seasons of change

The idea of rhythm is inherent to fashion and is visible in many ways. Winter requires a different attire to summer. Collections come out following the natural rhythm of the seasons, and even within a collection the idea of rhythm is an integral part of a designer's vocabulary.

There is a flow in a collection, an inherent logical development from one silhouette to another.

Rhythm is omnipresent even in a silhouette: by creating symmetry and a-symmetry a designer controls how it is observed, where the eye starts its exploration of the silhouette, the road it will travel over the body, the play with proportions and symmetry that dictate the rhythm of the observation, the focal points where the eye will linger, the cadence of the exploration.

Nature's rhythm is a driving force behind fashion. Nature grows about half of our materials,[10] and is a constant source of inspiration for many designers. During a major part of my career, I did not give nature, and how its an integral part of fashion a second thought. People who know me, are aware of my lack of green fingers; plants only survive in my office thanks to the intervention of my team.

In recent years it became apparent that I needed to learn more about agriculture. Being a vegan all my life, I have watched countless documentaries on animal agriculture, and it dawned on me, that to provide us with the number of plants we need for consumption and

---

10. Currently we wear about 60% of polyester and fossil fuel-based fibres; the remainder is grown as plants, fungi, animal fibres or trees.

products, there must be an equally big industry behind this, as there is behind animal production.

I became invested in understanding how my preferred fibres grow, where they grow, and what farmers do to enable the plants to grow them.

It was a learning curve to see how we have lost touch with natural growth and have demanded our suppliers to turn to artificial cultivation in big agricultural industrial settings – with its implied use of heavy chemicals and soil deletion – for all the fibres fashion uses. Leather and fur, often thought of as a by-product of the meat industry, are bred specifically to supply our need for them.

I began to learn about initiatives experimenting with alternative approaches, and their success stories. How organic cultivation is becoming more common in the textile supply chain; how regenerative farming practices are creating new ways of looking at old wisdom and creating a holistic perspective starting from nature's rhythm.

Thus, in order to assess your materials, and make informed choices about what fibres to choose, it is vital to understand how conventional cotton or flax grows before you can assess its impact. Only then can we acknowledge the importance of changing to alternatively grown crops or alternative materials.

Today, I can honestly say I know more about soil, soil regeneration, organic crops, sustainable forestry than ever before. And my knowledge, like those crops, keeps growing.

Yes, as a fashion designer, we need to understand agriculture, since we use the fruits of its labour. Material knowledge must start before identifying fibres and twists in yarn. Learn how and where your fibres grow, and what best farming practices you demand. Learn how we grow things and how we could grow things. What kind of cultivation can be positively beneficial to the rhythm of our natural world?

At the beginning of my brands design journey, my initial, unthinking impulse was to use only organic plant-based materials. It seemed logical, and I understood intuitively that organically grown cotton must have a much better footprint than its conventional counterpart.

Research supports my initial understanding: it might appear that organic farming is less effective if we judge it only by yield per acre. But in the long run, when we factor in other elements like soil and water quality, social wellbeing, etc. organic crops are much more beneficial to our planet's overall health and can provide long term yields that remain stable.[11]

Once I started to understand more about what nutrient and soil health meant, making choices about what fibres and textiles to use became much easier.

Knowing your fibres comes before knowing your fabrics.

What nutrients make our fabrics?

Any living organism is dependent on nutrients to survive, grow, and reproduce. Different types of organisms have different essential nutrients. Plants require more diverse minerals absorbed through their roots, plus carbon dioxide and oxygen absorbed through the leaves. Essential nutrients for animals are the energy sources, some of the amino acids that are combined to create proteins, a subset of fatty acids, vitamins, and certain minerals.

Each nutrient consumed by a living organism enters a metabolic cycle where it is converted into smaller molecules to release energy for its host. In the process, the nutrients become carbohydrates, lipids, proteins, and fermentation products and in their final stage of generating energy they become water and carbon dioxide.

---

11. While there is a debate about whether organic cotton uses more or less water, it has been proven that the overall pollution of water and soil by conventional cotton, compensates any shortcomings in the yield per acre of organic cotton.

Nutrients can be either organic or inorganic. Organic nutrients include, among other things, energy-providing compounds, vitamins, and carbon. Inorganic nutrients include the other chemicals, and metals like iron, bronze, selenium, and zinc. Fossil fuel is the result of the geological deposits of organic materials. The decay of plants and animals over many hundreds of millions of years, by compression and exposure to heat, are converted into petroleum, coal, natural gas, or heavy oils. So, fossil fuels are an organic nutrient at their origin, but by the transformation they undergo, become inorganic.

In the light of our thinking in biological and technical cycles it is vital to understand the distinction between organic and inorganic, as it implies how and where to source these nutrients, how to design with them and what kind of future life we should incorporate into our thinking of them.

Soil

A Japanese farmer, Masanobu Fukuoka, started experimenting in the late 1940s with regenerative farming techniques in his orchard in the prefecture of Ehime. His techniques are referred to as natural farming or do-nothing farming. At the core of his practice lies a profound belief in the powers of nature to grow and reproduce lavishly.

When he started his personal journey in his fields, he stopped ploughing, tilling, or using any herbicides/pesticides or fertilizer. Instead, he observed his orchard and implemented strategies he copied from wild nature, blending different vegetation, looking at plants that thrive in a dependency relationship and more.

His fields improved in fertility, structure, and in their ability to retain water.

But the most important takeaway from his farming methods was not the yield. As important as a harvest is, he found that all three methods of farming – natural, traditional, and chemical – yield comparable crop volumes. It might come as a surprise, but when a fertilized, pest-controlled field is compared to an organic natural one, in terms of yield they are approximately the same. In the early years of intro-duction, after the first application of GMO seeds, and sedating the field with fertilizers and pesticides, the crops will seemingly thrive, creating staggering quantities. But this effect will fade away after a couple of years, and as a drug addict, looking for the same experience as in the first year of use, farmers will need to keep using more and more chemicals to maintain the same results.

The reason behind this, lies in the topsoil. A farmer can enrich the soil in various ways: with fertilizer, by employing traditional farm-ing techniques, or by nurturing the soil in ways nature has always done. And the results of those different approaches could not be more divers.

The chemical farmer's soil becomes lifeless and depleted of its native fertility in a short time.[12] With traditional farming methods, the condition of soil over the years remains about the same; the yield is in direct proportion to the amount of compost and manure is put in.

Fukuoka on the contrary, saw the quality of the soil on his fields improve every season.

Topsoil is the upper layer of soil, the place where the highest concen-trations of organic matter and microorganisms thrive. It is composed of mineral particles, organic matter, water, and air and it holds nitro-gen that enables plants to build tissue, while also capturing carbon, to provide plants with the energy needed to grow.

---

12. Masanobu Fukuoka, The One-Straw Revolution, An Introduc-tion to Natural Farming. Pg. xxiv

Producing topsoil takes the earth significant time,[13] but we have not treated it with much respect or recognition over the last 150 years: take the Iowa prairie – it has lost 50% (about 20-25 cm) of its topsoil in the last 150 years. And this problem is not local to Iowa. It is estimated that the United States loses topsoil 10% faster than it can replenish while China and India are at rates of 30 to 40 times faster. With every inch of topsoil we lose, the soil will harvest about 6% less. Topsoil is lost due to erosion, and the impact of agricultural practices like nutrient degradation, soil salinity, and compaction, but the fact is that 95% of all food grown worldwide needs topsoil to grow.[14]

What is this fertile blanket of topsoil? In Iowa it is referred to as "black gold", and it is essentially thousands of years of prairie grass growth, death, and decomposition.

Active strategies for soil conservation are planting trees as wind barriers, preferring native plants for ground cover, no-till farming, crop rotation and soil hydration or irrigation.[15]

When soil is thriving, it can: absorb more carbon dioxide (vital since we love producing it); hold more water (so we can almost completely

---

13. It is estimated that it takes about 400-500 years to create one inch of topsoil. Renee Cho, Why Soil Matters. (Columbia Climate School, State of the Planet, April 12, 2012)

14. WWF, Soil Erosion and Degradation, overview, causes, impacts. Susan Cosier, The world needs topsoil to grow 95% of its food – but it's rapidly disappearing. (The Guardian, May 30, 2019) Richard Gray, Why soil is disappearing from farms. BBC, part of the Follow the Food series. (July 19, 2019) William McDonough & Michael Braungart, The Upcycle: Beyond Sustainability – Designing for Abundance. pg. 126

15. Kristen Ohlson, The Soil Will Save Us: How Scientists, Farmers and Foodies are Healing the Soil to Save the Planet. (New York: Rodale press, 2014) undefinedJohn Geisei, 10 Ways to Conserve Topsoil. (July 21, 2017)

stop watering our fields); and create stronger crops, making them less likely to fall victim to pests or other crop diseases.[16]

Organic

One might wonder why the experiments and discoveries of a Japanese farmer almost 80 years ago are relevant for sustainable fashion.

Most plant-based material receive a lot of negative feedback today for depleting the soil and consuming lavish amounts of water, not to mention polluting our waterways with pesticides, herbicides and the like. But this is only true for conventional agriculture and processing. Organic and regenerative practices have a whole different impact and even a positive effect on soil quality.

Ever since the rise of modern agriculture, worshipping monoculture and seed optimization, we have entered a highway of soil destruction. With each new harvest soil is depleted more and more. Fukuoka's work has inspired new generations of farmers and ecologists to look at nature as an ally rather than an enemy.

Organic farming is an agricultural system that originated in the early 20th century, as a direct reaction to the rapidly industrializing farming practices. Organic farming is "an integrated farming system that strives for sustainability, the enhancement of soil fertility and biological diversity while, with rare exceptions, prohibiting synthetic

---

16. "Grow a soft, fat rice plant in a flooded filed and you get a plant easily attacked by insects and disease. If "improved seed varieties are used, one must rely on the help of chemical insecticides and fertilizer. On the other hand, if you grow a small, sturdy plant in a healthy environment, these chemicals are unnecessary. Cultivate a flooded rice field with a plough or tractor and the soil becomes deficient of oxygen, the soil structure is broken down, earthworms and other small animals are destroyed, and the earth becomes hard and lifeless. Once this happens, the field must be turned every year. Masanobu Fukuoka, The One-Straw Revolution, An Introduction to Natural Farming. pg. 167-168

pesticides, antibiotics, synthetic fertilizers, genetically modified organisms, and growth hormones."[17].

Organic farming is something that for the food chain is quite mainstream today. In fibre and textile making organic farming is slowly becoming more and more common. The international Global Organic Textile Standard (GOTS) label is the most reliable and rigorous organic certificate. It advocates full transparency and traceability, requiring all those who handle the fibre, from farm to wardrobe, to be vetted. All who come in contact need to operate well within the organic standard they uphold. The requirements cover topics like water and waste management, chemical control, social standards and many more.

Beyond organic

The next revolution is that farmers are moving towards regenerative agricultural practices, which are embedded in the Fukuoka teachings.

It was Fukuoka's experience that "direct seeding non-cultivation will prove to be the best way. When we stop using weak, "improved" seed varieties, stop adding to much nitrogen to the soil, and reduce the amount of irrigation water so that strong roots could develop, diseases would all but disappear and chemical sprays would become unnecessary".[18]

---

17. Danielle Treadwell et al. What is Organic? (eOrganic, Jan. 22, 2009)

18. Masanobu Fukuoka, The One-Straw Revolution, An Introduction to Natural Farming. pg. 70

FARMING

CONVENTIONAL	ORGANIC
• Synthetic interventions for pest control & plant nutrition.	• Biodiversity to protect crops.
• Pesticides, herbicides, fungicides, fertilizers.	• Composting.
	• Crop rotation.
• Antibiotics in livestock.	• Companion planting.
• Tillage.	• Use natural fertilizers like compost, green manure or bone meal.
• Monocropping.	
• Soil conditioners.	• Fostering natural insect predators, etc.
• Mechanized transplantation.	• Antibiotics are severely restricted.
• Accelerated short period cultivation.	• No GMO.
AIMS:	• Grow local crops.
• Increase yield.	• Use local resources.
• Increase economic profit.	AIMS:
• Labor saving automation and mechanization.	• Reduce water consumption.
	• Reduce energy consumption.
	• Improve soil water holding capacity.
	• Eliminating synthetic chemical imput.
	• Reduce soil loss.
	• Create larger floral, faunal and microbiological biodiversity.
	• Increase soil organic matter protect human, animal and soil health.

REGENERATIVE

• Minimize soil disruption.
• Keep soil covered with plants.
• Plant diverse crops.
• Planned grazing.

AIMS:
• To foster the ecosystem.
• To sequester carbon.

The soil degrades over time and becomes infertile.

The soil replenishes and becomes more and more fertile.

Regenerative agriculture[19] builds on the principles and practices of organic farming to help communities – and soil – thrive. It simply takes organic farming to the next level. It combines local traditional farming systems that have stood the test of time with the knowledge gained from organic farming to provide benefits beyond avoiding poisoning the ground and water in which we grow our crops.

If all farming would go this route, it would bring about a complete change to the economic, ecological, and social structures of society and the environmental challenges with which we are confronted today.

The impact of regenerative farming is vast. Regenerative agriculture practices farming and grazing techniques that reverse climate change by rebuilding the soil's organic matter and restoring degraded soil biodiversity. The results can be seen in carbon drawdown and improving the water cycle while making the farmer, his family, and the world a healthier place.

Thus, when we change the way we grow our crops, we change our food[20], we change our society, we change our values.

The complete set of practices takes into consideration the geography and topography of the land, the condition of the soil, its structure, texture, and drainage, exposure to sunlight, insect relationships, the variety of seed used, the method of cultivation – truly an infinite variety of factors. It represents a genuinely holistic approach.

---

19. Rodale institute, Regeneration International, IFOAM organics International are all great places to learn more about the ideas behind regenerative agriculture.

20. I use food here in the broadest interpretation of the word. Food for humans, animals, clothing, and anything else we grow our base building blocks for. France is one of the biggest producers of flax, yet 90% of its crop goes to the chemical and pharmaceutical industry.

Human civilization has reached a point where careless destruction of nature and planet has become the new normal. Animals becoming extinct, desertification all over the world, water poisoning and soil exhaustion of soil. But we must remember, we did not create nature, regardless of how well we understand the chemical build-up of a banana, regardless of how thoroughly we grasp the atom construction of a fibre.

We can restore what we destroyed, but, this will take time and patience, and there is no instant fix.

If we create new, we are doing this blindly, with little understanding of the broader impact of our actions. Nature has spent thousands of years and trial and error to create functioning systems. Thinking we can mimic this and add to her universe without hiccups is pure hubris. Humans are capable of inventing and creating systems, yet overseeing the possible implications of our actions is incredibly co mplex.[21]

Every element on our earth is interconnected, and any adaptation will require a new balance to be found. When we introduce new species, others will change or disappear; if we eliminate them, different vegetation might invade or mutate. Change is a normal part

---

21. We developed ways of extracting nuclear energy, yet we fail to have proper solutions for the waste generated, and when things go wrong, they go catastrophically wrong. We have not yet developed ways of dealing with the results of human error in a non-invasive way.

of life on earth, but moving too fast, with little understanding of the total complexity turns out to be disastrous every time.[22]

As recently as 50 years ago we discovered the role of keystone species[23] : organisms that help define an entire ecosystem. Without their presence, the ecosystem would be dramatically different or cease to exist altogether. Their functioning is a subtle reminder of the intangible web that connects us all.

The tragedy of unfounded human arrogance is illustrated by our belief that pest-resistant crops are the optimized version of nature which benefit the world and our consumption needs.

In light of living within nature, thinking in terms of circular design, a regenerative point of view is indispensable, and should be intertwined with socio-environmental feedback loops.

---

22. The bee population has dropped more than 60% since the 1940s. When healthy bees are fed pollen filled with fungicides, insecticides, and other agricultural chemicals, they are more likely to be infected by Nosema ceranae, a parasitic microsporidian fungus associated with widespread death of honeybees. Bees are perfectly adapted to pollinate, helping plants grow, breed, and produce food. They do so by transferring pollen between flowering plants and so keep the cycle of life turning. It is estimated that one third of the food that we consume each day relies on pollination mainly by bees.

23. Zoologist Robert T. Paine introduced the concept in 1969, as species which have a disproportionately large effect on its natural environment. Today we recognize five main categories of keystone species: predators (like wolves, sea otters and sharks); prey (diverse, from krill and kelp to snow shoe hares); mutualists (two or more species that engage in reciprocally vital interactions like pollinators, bees, or specific plants that feed hummingbirds to spread pollen to create more plants); ecosystem engineers (they create, maintain, or modify the landscape like elephants or beavers); and certain plants like the Sonoran Desert's Saguaro Cactus, providing critical food source and/or shelter for other species.

Holistic Thinking to Facilitate Choices

On 7 December 1972 the crew of the Apollo 17 spacecraft took an image of earth, today known as the Blue Marble. Is has become one of the most reproduced images in human history.

At about 29.000 kilometres (18,000 miles) from the earth's surface, the enormity of the earth in relation to each of us becomes vividly clear. Understanding our planet's fragile beauty is best understood when we see the whole, and not just one little aspect that concerns us.

When one thing changes, it is bound to influence all. This implies that every little alteration you bring to your practice will have an impact and an influence beyond your actions. It can create a ripple effect. It holds the power to create a magnitude beyond our imagination.

This is exactly how fashion works: by creating a new form, offering a new, better, improved version, a cascade effect of people starting to desire this and taking over the market.

By designing a changed form, or by employing new practices, you can offer a new choice, a new reality. And in fashion, people crave the new. Demand thus grows until it reaches a tipping point, where even big companies accept the new norm.[24]

---

24. Even Primark now advertises their organic and other positive efforts. Clearly this is for economic gain, but from a business perspective, it would be economic suicide today to not have a sustainability program. Schiaparelli's presentation of big cats as normal decoration on clothing had the same effect, it created a new visual norm, not a desirable one, but still a new norm, that hunted big cats make acceptable dress decoration. Visually there was no way of telling that the original big cat dresses used fake heads. It just launched a new acceptable visual norm, in times that all big cats are fighting for their survival.

Today eating meat is the norm, but studies have shown, that if meat eaters are placed in situations where vegan is the norm, change is adamant. Most people like to belong to the majority, adhering to the norm. So, by changing the norm, by having fashion trendsetters demanding and pushing change, a paradigm shift can occur and the new normal will please both humans and the planet.

Choosing opportunistically

A weed is simply a plant considered undesirable in a particular situation, with no recognition of its inherent virtues. In Belgium, like many places in the world, people in their private gardens, and public spaces are obsessed with clean, neat grass lawns. This is disastrous for biodiversity and insects.

Additionally, creating and maintaining this requires serious human intervention to prevent all other elements from growing. In our attempt to control and regulate nature, we have completely lost her.

Every spring I pass beautiful wild fields with wildflowers, and it's just a matter of days till the city official comes and cuts it all away, spraying and killing any restoration efforts by nature.[25] The distinction made between weeds and desired crops looks arbitrary in this light.

All plants are weeds and not weeds at the same time; by our authoritarian preference of one crop over many other crops we create a situation that is no longer capable of operating in a natural rhythm.

When practicing good holistic farming, nature and farmer strive for the same: abundance. Seeking shelter from nature with pesticides / herbicides / pest control / GMO is trying to defy or improve nature.

---

25. One way of being part of the change is joining No Mow May. First initiated by Plantlife is rapidly picking up popularity all over Europe and North America. By not cutting laws in the month of May by citizens and local governments, bees and other early pollinators are given temporary more habitat and forage.   undefined

Farmer and nature are no longer operating as one in a natural cycle of day and night, seasonal change, and constant regeneration.

Humanity has historically lived in symbiotic relation to nature. Nature was for the longest time our capital and currency in one.

Currency is something you can use or trade with, and then it is gone and you have nothing left. Capital can go on forever with endless resourcefulness, multiplying, bearing fruit, providing you with more energy and abundance for many centuries.[26]

Today we see and use nature as a currency, something we use, and deplete. Not something we responsibly manage, foster and use.

Burned and scorned fields illustrate the complete disconnect we have with nature. Burning what she provides shows a total lack of respect and appreciation of what she gives. We are simply dispersing and contaminating our earthly capital. We're treating what should be capital like currency.

As a fashion designer, design your natural fibres as part of a perpetual cycle of use and reuse, so their inert qualities are respected.

Design to nurture, connect, cooperate, and regenerate. Aim for a qualitative production and cyclic use of the planet's multiple produce.

The end goal is endless resources and a positive footprints.

---

26. Hernando de Soto, The Mystery of Capital: Why capitalism Triumphs in the West and Fails Everywhere Else. (New York: Basic Books, 2000)

Six

Space, a social environment

Human hands make all cloth.

I T IS SO EASY not to recognise your own privilege. You theoretically know it's there, but that does not make you feel it. Everybody reading this book has some kind of privilege over others. It might not be obvious, you might not even realise it, but many people around the globe are less privileged than you. One could argue whether we are privileged, or others undervalued. I would argue the latter, but for our next investigation it has little importance either way.

We live in a world of inequality. And historically the lesser privileged in society work in textiles.

The textile industry occupies a permanent space in our society. It employs over 430 million people worldwide and is the primary source of income for many worker families in low-income social groups. The Fairtrade Foundation estimates that as many as 100 million households are directly engaged in cotton production and that as many as 300 million people work in the complex total cotton industry.[1] They are often invisible, under-paid and underprivileged.

---

1. It really depends on how you count. Do you only focus on the cotton production, but cotton is not only used in the textile industry. And do you count all textile or only the fashion part? Textile is used for other purposes too. In any case 430 million is a very mild estimate. "An estimated 350 million people work in the cotton sector when family labour, farm labour and workers in connected services such as transportation, ginning, baling and storage are taken into account." Fairtrade Foundation. Cotton Farmers. 2019

We know that about one out of eight workers worldwide is involved in the broad textile industry.[2]

This by no means implies that all work in fashion, or even in garments. A lot of textiles is made for other industries, like the automotive industry (car seats), the aerospace industry (spacesuits), medical membranes, etc.

About 75 to 80% of all textile workers are women.

The International Labour Organisation estimates that, by their definition, over 21 million people[3] were in some form of slavery in 2016. 14.2 million people are in forced economic labour, exploited in the private sector such as domestic work, construction, agriculture, and the textile industry. About 2.2 million people are forced to work by the state, again often for the textile industry (prison work) or rebel military groups. Up until 2018, Colorado had an exception on its constitutional ban on slavery for prisoners. Many USA states still force their prisoners to work today as modern slaves.

Child labour in textile processing units

Estimates are that one million children perform child labour, many of them in the textile industry.

Child labour is defined as any child working under the age of 15. Of the victims of child labour 48% are a shocking 5-11 years old[4]. In

---

2. World Bank, 2017, Total Labour Force. The total labour force is estimated to be 3.4 billion people, and about 430 million of them are believed to work in textile.

3. International Labour Organization (ILO) & Walk Free Foundation, Methodology of the global estimates of modern slavery: Forced labour and forced marriage (2017)

4. International Labour Organization (ILO) & Walk Free Foundation, Global Estimates of Child Labour. Results and Trends, 2012 - 2016 (2017)

many cases, this work involves long hours, unsafe working conditions, and low wages.

The vulnerability of children in child labour made it necessary for the United Nations to issue a special protection, in the form of the 'Convention on the Rights of the Child', which came into effect in 1990[5]. Within the Convention, children are guaranteed a right to education and a right to play and leisure time. These two promises of childhood are most at risk of being lost when young people engage in child labour.

In considering why child labour is so prevalent in fashion, it is important to understand the low-skill nature of most garment industry processes. Children can often be better physically suited for the work than adults, having smaller hands for more intricate work such as beading or sequin making. This is a critical reason why children are so heavily employed in picking cotton in particular[6]. One example is Uzbekistan, with a cotton industry workforce of +2 million people, reports indicate that they have managed for the first time in 2021 to clear their supply chain from forced labour and child labour[7].

5. UNICEF, The United Nations Convention on the Rights of the Child. Entry into force September 2, 1990. (London: Unicef, 2010)

6. Josephine Moulds, Child labour in the fashion supply chain. Where, why and what can be done. (The Guardian, Jan. 15, 2015)

7. International Labour Organization (ILO) Activist welcome progress towards eradication of forced labour, child labour in Uzbekistan. Press release (April 3, 2019) Uzbek cotton is free from systemic child labour and forced labour. Press release (March 1, 2022)

Child labour and forced labour often appear simultaneous.[8] What links these countries, and all areas where child labour is most prevalent, is a high rate of poverty combined with gender inequality and barriers to free and accessible education[9].

The fashion industry needs to take responsibility for its contribution to the systemic poverty of those working in its supply chain. By consistently driving down the cost of clothing, fashion brands perpetuate a situation where workers earn extremely low pay, meaning that parents have few other options but to send their children to work. Considering that the vast majority of garment workers are women and working mothers, ensuring a living wage, and eliminating any gender wage gap for the people that make our clothes is key to keeping children safe and in school.[10]

The conditions that people face whilst working in the fashion industry keep them trapped in poverty, and their children are needed to supplement the family income.

For the moment the fashion industry as we know it depends on cheap labour and uneducated workers and unless we change this fundamental injustice and imbalance between the rich and poor, it will remain because we profit and gain products on their backs.

---

8. Somo, Fact Sheet; Child labour in the textile & garment industry. (Amsterdam: Stichting Onderzoek Multinationale Ondernemingen, 2014) The most at-risk countries for child labour in the fashion supply chain are Bangladesh, China, Egypt, India, Pakistan, Thailand and till 2021 Uzbekistan.

9. Somo, Flawed Fabrics, The abuse of girls and women workers in the South Indian textile industry. (Amsterdam, SOMO, 2014)

10. Institute for Sustainability Leadership (CISL), Shift, Business Fights Poverty and University of Cambridge. J. Nelson, et al. The case for living wages: how paying living wages improves business performance and tackles poverty. (Cambridge: University of Cambridge, May 16, 2022)

We created our world from textiles[11]

I want to dedicate this chapter to all those invisible human hands that make the textiles and clothes that shape our world.

Everything that is made is done so somewhere, by somebody. This seems self-explanatory but is often overlooked in textile.

When we purchase a garment, this is made, along the full production line, by people.

If you lay that information next to the price the final consumer pays for a garment, it just does not add up. We are not paying the price of the work it represents. This example works for any garment, but let's look at that wardrobe basic everywhere, the humble t-shirt. The seed, planted by a farmer most likely in India, Brazil, China, or the Southern United States, is most likely bought from one of four multinational concerns that sell GMO seeds, fertilisers and pesticides. That seed is cultivated, harvested, and then seeds and chaff are separated in the ginning process. The spinner will then card, spin, comb and blend the cotton fibres into yarn. From there, the yarn will travel to the knitter or weaver who will make a textile from the fibre.

---

11. Kassia St Clair, The Golden Thread, How fabric changed history. (London: John Murray, 2018) Pg. 1-18 The author points out that we are born into this world, into a blanket, and leave this world in a burial shroud. Our language is saturated by textile references like a thread of hope, the veil of oblivion, etc. the importance of textile in human society cannot be overestimated.

Worldmap of all the countries Infantium Victoria, my company, knowingly operates in.

Countries we work and communicate directly with.

Countries we assume to source from, but we have no direct contact.

A series of treatments is released on the fabric, called wet processing. This includes washing, heating, and treating it with a long list of chemicals to dye, print, and or bleach it. It might receive a fire-retardant coating, or a coating to make it softer, or change its performance.

Next stop for the fabric is the cutting and assembly factory. Here the parts will be cut out and the t shirt will be assembled, sewn, trimmed and checked for quality. Then it is once more ready to travel to the next location: warehouse or wholesalers storage before being dispatched to the final store clerk or waiting in an online business's warehouse until it can be united with the final customer.

Every step of the way, a long list of people is involved in the making of this garment. Add to this list the designer, pattern-maker, distributors, sourcing agents, and middlemen who broker the buying and selling of elements, and the marketing team. The income distribution of any purchased t-shirt is flawed. Those that spent the most time on the garment are paid the least. The breakdown of the price build-up reveals that the mark up towards the end of the value chain is disproportionate compared to the beginning of the value chain. Farmers, spinners, and weavers are not compensated in the same way as designers or shop assistants. Their skills and time are highly undervalued in today's pricing, especially if you know how long it takes and how many hands are involved to grow and make every t-shirt.[12]

The question is, whether these labour-intensive t-shirts can or should cost €30?

When we are rooting for better practices along the value chain[13], we need to consider the bottom end of our value chain first. What kind of spaces and places would you want your clothes to be made in?

The real price of any garment is that there is a need to keep people and countries poor, to supply our everlasting hunger for more and cheap. And we should realise profoundly what cheap means: it is the

---

12. Of course, by making volume the making time of one garment drops drastically. Making one t shirt, from scratch, will take about 1 hour in patterning, 20 min in cutting, and 1 hour in sewing, if all the machines are ready and threaded with the right colour and tension. In the factories, the sewing time of one single t-shirt might be reduced to 2 minutes. But only if the workers all are doing one precise action, and there is a chain of over 1000 pieces happening. But that time still does not encompasses the growing and making of the textiles, the designer or brand work to develop the first prototype and all actions happening after the t-shirt is sewn. Shipping to the final country of sales, the shop, the marketing,

13. A value chain is a step-by-step business model for transforming a product or service from idea to reality. In the fashion industry, this consists of all the elements between the anticipated customers' known or unknown needs for textile related products and the ability of the business concept creators to realise this in the most cost-effective way.

exploitation of men, women and children in countries and places where they don't have any means to speak up without losing their sole income.

Complexity of the industry

The fashion industry is particularly complex due to its current configuration. Most major fashion brands work with hundreds if not thousands of suppliers, sub-suppliers, and garment factories at any given time. Most brands do not own their own manufacturing and are dependent on textile suppliers and factories to which they outsource the manufacturing of their products. Monitoring this in terms of worker conditions and environmental impact is challenging.

The influence of the textile industry can hardly be overestimated.[14] It transgresses all borders, of nations, state laws, age, ethnicity, gender, etc. It occupies an extensive space in our globalised society.

In fashion the concept of equality is in many regards problematic. The people who are making fashion, in poor countries, are mostly young women, who are treated with very little sense of equality. The fact that prices are still pressed down by big corporations upon poor communities with very little tools to fight this is a harsh reality we are facing constantly.

Rich consuming countries in the world monopolise the majority of all grown and made produce in the world. Compared to other commodities, clothing has seen a very slow increase in price, making it comparatively cheaper and cheaper. We are now selling them at a price that in no way represents their actual cost.[15]

---

14. The sheer size of the industry is estimated today to be the fifth biggest in the world, behind consumer electronics, commercial real estate, fast food restaurants and HR recruitment services. Ibis world. Global biggest Industries by Employment in 2023.

15. Imram Amed et al., The State of Fashion 2023 (London,: McKinsey&Company & BOF, 2022)

We can only consume the volumes we do because we safeguard economic boundaries. The current model thrives on oppression and cannot sustain itself without the misconduct we see around the globe today. If we want to abolish slavery and human exploitation, we need to think out of the box. Fixing our current ways will not be sufficient since it is built on pillars of human and environmental suffering.

For me as a female designer, working in Belgium, imagining a work situation with constant discrimination and violence, and visualising these numbers remains very abstract. And it is hard to grasp the day-to-day reality most of these people live and work in.

The first time I felt what privilege entails was during my first job. I was working in Antwerp, Belgium, for the small independent brand Jurgi Persoons. He is one of those designers that has the almost magical power of creating clothes that make you feel and move differently when you put them on. They give you flair.

During sales season, I accompanied the team to the Paris showroom. Each day was the same, sitting in the showroom for 10 hours, waiting for shop-owners to pass by. They would browse through the collection hanging on display to select what they wanted to order for their shops. I was fresh out of high-school, and it was all exciting to me. Each morning we would go over the agenda to prepare for the people who had made appointments.

One day, we had a big customer writing big orders coming in, and our instructions were clear. The silhouettes we would present should definitely have little bare skin showing, and cover elbows and knees, as they only bought modest designs. This would be a challenge since almost all the dresses were sheer chiffon and what they required was not really the season's aesthetic.

The salesgirl and I started pre-selecting outfits to dress our showroom model. The collection was a mix of tartans and checks and Jurgi was adamant that even though we could build matching outfits, this was not the idea. So, we assembled a first outfit of pants with a long sleeved shirt and a sweater hung loosely over the shoulders, and dressed our showroom model. In this way, when the customer arrived, they could already get an idea of how our garments could fit their needs.

The moment arrived and the customer entered the showroom. Immediately there was a fuss. Pants without a skirt or dress would be unacceptable. And was everything mismatched? Were we colour- and print-blind?

They instructed us immediately to start again, but this time, matching everything and at least with a skirt or dress. While Jurgi was pacing backstage, we started again. Skirt, long sleeved sweater, all neatly matching, expressly the opposite of Jurgi's vision. Again, we received a complaint: this was really not viable. They client seemed progressive enough, dressed in the latest fashion, yet they were demanding that we would put pants under every sheer dress. A silhouette needed to be created out of at least five garments, layering and covering the model's entire body.

They mentioned that in their country it would never sell otherwise. Once we understood what they wanted we set to work, dressing the model again. Finally, we got it right and they began the process of ordering. Five of each garment they saw, ordering the full outfit we presented. They didn't even bother to browse the racks of clothing. They insisted we kept dressing the model, assembling and showing them full outfits. Each silhouette assembled according to their wishes, ignoring the aesthetic vision behind the collection. Usually, our other customers did not buy the entire outfits we presented, as they preferred to create their own outfits and browse the racks looking for the shapes and styles they liked.

This customer seemed to enjoy and appreciate our work, watching us running around, showing them things, bringing them drinks and fresh fruit. My sales colleague was writing the full order, I was selecting new outfit after new outfit, and the model was showing each and every one of them. All was going well and then they suddenly abruptly said they were finished and demanded to speak to the salesperson.

Again, we did not understand as their salesperson was sitting in front of them. She had been welcoming them, discussing different styles, and taking down their full order. But then they got agitated, raised their voice, and demanded to speak to the man in charge. There was no way, a few girls, like us, good for bringing them coffee and wearing the clothes, would be the ones to close a deal with them. They where not about to discuss money, delivery terms or anything business with us. They demanded to see *the salesman in charge.*

At this point, panic ensued, as besides our designer Jurgi, we were a team of only girls that day. And Jurgi's job was clearly not to close the orders; he was already stressed enough, praying we would sell enough to last another season. But there was no way of talking to the customer at this point. They shouted demanding to do proper business with somebody qualified, meaning a man, or they would walk. Left without any other option, Jurgi walked in to settle and sign what my sales colleague told him to.

It was the first time in my life that I felt that I might not be qualified, or good enough to do something, because of my gender. And I knew I could not say anything, without risking losing that customer. So, each of us in the room, at that moment chose to remain quiet and accept the clear gender discrimination in favour of our sales order.

But life continued, and I put it aside as an anomaly. Attaching this experience only to this customer, and nothing else.

If all are to be equal

On 26th August 1789, the French National Constituent Assembly issued the Déclaration des Droits de l'Homme et du Citoyen (Declaration of the Rights of Man and the Citizen).[16]

This document was inspired by the Enlightenment philosophers and represented a core definition of the values of the French Revolution.

---

16. The original draft is an annex to the 12 August report, the 2nd lengthier version was written but never formally adopted. Archives parlementaires, Déclaration des Droits de l'Homme et du Citoyen. 1e série, tome VIII, , p. 431)

It had an immediate, long-lasting and major impact on the development of popular conceptions of Individual Liberty and Democracy worldwide.[17]

Article four states that "Liberty consist of being able to do anything that does not harm others; thus, the exercise of the natural rights of every man or woman has no bound other than those that guarantee other members of society the enjoyment of these same rights."

Article six states that the law "must be the same for all, whether it protects or punishes. All citizens, being equal in its eyes, shall be equally eligible to all high offices, public positions, and employments, according to their ability, and without other distinction than that of their virtues and talents."

Since the French Revolution, this concept of equality has spread like wildfire, taking over western and eventually global thinking leading to the United Nations Declaration of Universal Human Rights.[18] We all are equal because we all are rational human beings. We also all share the same proportions, making us all equal, non-superior over others, regardless of our visual differences.

In 1947, the UN defined Human Rights for all Human Beings, including the right to live free from violence, slavery, and discrimination; to be educated; to own property; to vote; and to earn a fair and equal wage.

---

17. This document, together with the 1689 English Bill of Rights, the 1776 United States Declaration of Independence and the 1789 United States Bill of Rights, inspired in large part the 1948 United Nations Universal Declaration Of Human Rights. See www.un.org for the full text. Douglas K. Stevenson (1987), American Life and Institutions, (Stuttgart: 1987) pg. 34 Jeffrey Kopstein (ed.), . (Cambridge: Cambridge University Press, 2014). pg.72

18. Gerda Smets et al. Beeldspel, Ruimtelijk inzicht en beelddenken. (Delft: Delfste Universitaire Press, 1994) pg 29 translation by the author.

That declaration is about 70 years old, yet today we still feel traces of fundamental inequality throughout societies around the globe. And those most at risk of being treated as second-class citizens often are producing fibres, yarn, textiles and clothes.

Women's liberation by textile

The relation between textile and women's labour has been ongoing and complex since the beginning of time.

Since the inception of human and textile history, thread and textile making were regarded as female occupations, perhaps because they could be done at home, with an eye on the offspring. It was also a job that could easily be interrupted and resumed at will.

> "Transforming fibres into thread was time-consuming and highly skilled work, performed by hand by many millions of women until the spread of mechanisation following the Industrial revolution."[19]

The growing of fibres and roaring of sheep was often a men's job, but the transformation mostly fell upon the women of the communities. In many societies throughout history women living independently, widows, unmarried girls, and others from all layers of society practiced the art of spinning, weaving, lacemaking, embroidery work and other textile embellishment to support the family income, or to provide themselves with a livelihood. It provided economic power and a level of independence. It would not come with equal remuneration, but it could keep women out of poverty if they possessed skills in textile related crafts.

---

19. Kassia St Clair, The Golden Thread, How fabric changed history. (London: John Murray, 2018) pg. 13

Women equal to men

Today gender is often a defining factor in the career of a fashion worker.

The Human Rights Declaration proclaims that all humans share the same rights, responsibilities, and opportunities. It implies that the interests, needs and priorities of all people are taken into consideration, still recognising the diversity of different groups. Equality between women and men is seen both as a human rights issue and as a precondition for, and indicator of, sustainable people-centred development[20].

A 2019 World Bank report found that just six countries give women and men equal legal rights. This is an improvement from a decade ago, in which the report found that no country guaranteed full legal equality.[21] Reality in factories around the globe illustrate these numbers. Women are still treated legally, economically, and socially very differently from men.

For the majority, the factories we at Infantium Victoria work with are owned and led by men. But most of those making our clothes are women. There are two exceptions: our German factory is owned by a woman and all workers are women, and our Indian block printing unit, is led by a woman with mostly male workers. Globally speaking, these are black swans in the textile supply chain.

For centuries, across most cultures, communities, religions, economies and different political structures, women's status has been that of men's subordinates, thus giving men a dominant position. Today men still benefit from better wages, fewer domestic

---

20. European Institute for Gender Equality. Concepts and Definitions. (2019)

21. Via Future learn, United Nations. Dispatch: Only Six Countries In the World Have Full Gender Equality in the Work Place. (Mar 8, 2019)

responsibilities, and higher levels of education in the greater part of the world.[22]

Globally, women are estimated to earn 77% of what men earn, although these figures understate the real extent of gender pay gaps, particularly in developing countries where informal self-employment is prevalent,[23] and almost 40% of women in wage employment do not have access to social protection[24].

In 2019, the right of everyone to work free from violence and harassment was agreed in an international treaty and will be progressively ratified by the 187 International Labour Organisation member states. In 2021, when the treaty came into force, only 6 countries ratified the treaty, leaving millions of women vulnerable on a daily basis[25].

The global fashion industry depends heavily on women in their supply chain, on the shop floors and within their companies. In the 2019 Fashion Transparency Index which covers 200 of the world's biggest fashion brands and retailers, just over one-third of the brands disclosed that they are supporting women's empowerment projects for garment workers. However, only three brands published data on the prevalence of gender-based violations in supplier facilities.[26]

22. Hans Rösling, Factfulness: Ten Reasons We're Wrong About the World and Why Things Are Better Than You Think. (New York: Flatiron, 2018)

23. United Nations, Women: Equal pay for work of equal value. (2019)

24. International Labour Organization (ILO), Violence and Harassment Convention (Geneva: ILO, 2019) and Women at Work, trends 2016. (Geneva: ILO, 2019)

25. WORLD Policy Analysis Centre, Preventing gender-based workplace discrimination and sexual harassment: new data on 193 countries. (Los Angeles: WORLD 2017)

26. Fashion Revolution, Fashion Transparency Index 2019 (Fashion Revolution, 2019)

If society at large does not change its devaluing behaviour towards women, it is very hard for the day-to-day work situation for women in factories to improve, but not impossible. In many factories women receive a lower pay for the same work, but also, on the factory floors, they perform the lowest grade work and do the lowest paid, most vulnerable jobs. They move fibres, check yarn, place cones on spinning machines, move fabric, cut it, and sew it in the assembly line.

For the most part, supervisors, pattern-masters, master tailors are all men.

Promoting women's economic empowerment will not only benefit women, but it will also have an enormous effect on their families[27] impacting the lives of their children, and on how society treats them. A factory that starts paying women equally will create a direct impact on the women's lives and their social status and independence. There are factories that make sure every female worker on her first day opens her own bank account, where only she will have access to her salary.

For one of my designer customers, I was sent on a trip to a South-Asian country, about twelve years ago. They had visited first and was inspired by the local craftsmen to make a collection fully embroidered with French knots. My job was to launch and oversee the work.

My first stop was the agency hired to make the embroidery. Their office had a few embroidery frames set up, and three men happily demonstrated all the possibilities and options available. It dawned on me, that these three men, in the nicely air-conditioned space could never produce the volume we needed. So where was our production really going to take place? After days of hard negotiations, the head of the office finally granted me permission to visit the actual workshops. It turned out that these three men were the embroidery unit managers. I was never intended to set foot on their actual working floor.

---

27. https://www.worldvision.com.au/womens-empowerment/

My client during their visit, had happily accepted the idea that all their embroidery was made in this clean, air-conditioned, light space. Reality looked very different. Most units I visited were dirty, dark, and cramped with workers. One particular unit left a lasting impression. I was brought to a space with 20 people working *and* living in a room not bigger than 20 square meters, in the toxic fumes of some treatment they performed on the embellishment. I could not breath, and we immediately stopped all work with them.

We relaunched with another agency, and visited the various, much cleaner, healthier workspaces almost daily. During one of those days, I noticed that one of the craftsmen was embroidering a particular panel with way too many red threads; it needed to become a gradient, slowly moving from red to beige, and the transition was way to abrupt as they were making it. I tried to explain, that I wanted more beige, less red.

The young man kept nodding his head, saying; "No, it should be like this, the Mister said so". No matter what I said, I could not change his mind. Other workers joined the discussion and tried to explain to me that the Mister said it should be exactly like this. The workers refused to accept my corrections or change their course of action. The Mister said? What Mister? I was the lead client on site for this project. There was no Mister.

Feeling that I had no other option, I turned to my male driver, and asked him to intervene. He explained that we needed more beige, a softer transition in the embroidery, without telling them that I wanted this; he simply instructed what needed to happen. And suddenly it was no problem to change. In the minds of all these craftsmen, working for me, it was simply impossible for them to imagine that a woman could oversee such an important decision.

Promoting more women, to lead the team, to lead the factory floor, and paying them equally is one of the only ways this perception can change. Lead by example.

Unfortunately, this was not a one-off incident, and I could not then, and still cannot today, dismiss it as an anomaly. I have experienced it on factory floors, negotiating with factory owners, shop owners and craftsmen at every turn.

For women working in factories under male management and supervision, making any complaint or demand about equality is a fight against the deep-rooted idea that they are not, and cannot be equal.

All men are equal?

Since the French Revolution the idea that all humans are equal and should be treated as such has grown, from only being applicable to free men, then including women, then abolishing the idea of slavery and serfdom. So why do we still see modern day slavery?

Slavery and its establishment have been an ongoing historic battle. As early as 6th century BC Athenian citizens formerly enslaved were freed by Solon, the Greek lawgiver.[28] From this moment onward there has been worldwide a seesaw motion, abolishing debt bondage, slavery, establishing free peasantry and subsequently reinstating slavery.

The Qin dynasty in 221 – 206 BC eliminated landowning aristocracy including the abolition of slavery and discouraging serfdom, only to be overthrown with many of its laws overturned immediately after.

Throughout human history, laws against human exploitation and slavery have been implemented and subsequently abolished. Communities found other populations to control and enslave. Countries like Ireland banned slavery in the 5th century, only to reinstate it in the 9th century. Some laws merely prohibited the trade in slaves, or the transport of slaves; certain countries only excepted the trade of Christian, or Muslim slaves; others only prohibited the sale of heathens as slaves.

---

28. Aristotle, Constitution of the Athenians, Athenaion Politeia 12. 4, quoting Solon

In 1926 the Convention to Suppress the Slave Trade and Slavery was agreed by the League of Nations. This was the first time that, over the borders of nations, a statement was made that it was universally unacceptable to dominate and own other people and exploit them. It took many countries decades to put it into effect or ratify it - some as late as 2008.[29]

Today modern day slavery still exists as institutional slavery. Estimates range from around 21 million[30] to 46 million, depending on the methods and the definition of slavery being used. [31]

Industrial Revolution as a textile revolution

The textile *industry* historically got kickstarted during the industrial revolution in the 18th century. One could even say that the textile industry was one of the leading industries that drove industrialisation. Since the arrival of Columbus in America, trade became more and more reliant on free labour, hence slavery, and free land.

The newly established and large-scale plantations desperately needed cheap labour to make them profitable.[32] Between 1500 and 1800, over eight million people were transported from Africa to the Americas by the Spanish, Portuguese, French, British, Dutch, and Danish to serve as slaves and work the land.

---

29. Kazakhstan was the last of 99 countries that have committed to participate in the convention and its subsequent Protocol.

30. International Labour Organisation (ILO) operates with this estimate. The ILO is a United Nations agency, whose mandate is to advance social and economic justice through setting International Labour Standards. It was founded in 1919 under the League of Nations, and is the first and oldest specialised agency of the UN.

31. Walk Free Foundation, The Global Slavery Index 2018. (2018)

32. Kassia St Clair, The Golden Thread, How fabric changed history. Pg.168-169

Exploitation and oppression are deeply rooted in the historic development of the textile industry.

During almost every era in history, textile has been used as an important trading commodity. And the slave trade between Africa and the Americas was no different, furled by the cotton trade. Merchants would often pay for their slaves in Africa by means of cotton -- cotton which was grown by these same slaves in the Americas. To fuel the slave trade, Europe needed more and more cotton to pay for its inhuman practice, creating a demand for greater and faster extraction and processing of cotton fibres.

In India the growing, weaving and extracting of cotton was happening on a big scale, widely dominating the market since ancient times, making the finest of qualities yarn and textile, in huge volumes.

As American cotton became the cheaper option on the market, it was vital to optimise a processing line that could keep up with the stream of cotton fibres produced, to compete with the Indian supply. Workers in one part of the world were pitted against those in another, with new trade routes opening up cheaper sources of cotton and thus saving time, money, and land for other more profitable uses.

A steady stream of new British technological developments made spinning and weaving faster, more efficient, and cheaper. It made it possible to overthrow the Indian domination of cotton extraction and processing. In the US, the South's plantations pumped cheap cotton into Britain's textile factories.

An initial innovation, significantly enhancing speed and productivity, was the flying shuttle, invented by John Kay in 1733. In previous handlooms, a shuttle was thrown or passed through the threads by hand, and wide fabrics required two weavers seated at each side of the fabric, passing the shuttle between them. The flying shuttle was propelled from one side of the loom to the other, dragging the weaving thread with it, back and forth. The speed of weaving increased so drastically that it took four spinners to keep up with one weaver.[33]

The speed of the spinning process had to be drastically improved to supply the newly created demand for more thread. The Spinning Jenny, developed by James Hargreaves in 1764 catered to this new need. By turning a single wheel, one could now spin eight spindles of threads at once, a number that was later increased to 80. This was much more efficient than the popular spinning wheel that until then could only make one spindle of thread at a time.

The Spinning Jenny soon was replaced by the Water Frame, invented by Richard Arkwright, that was too big to be operated by hand. It was powered by a water wheel, producing volumes of stable yarn with much less human labour required.

In 1779, Samuel Crompton combined the Spinning Jenny and the Water Frame to create a machine known as "Crompton's mule," which produced large amounts of fine, strong yarn.[34]

Equality in worker suffering

The workers in British factories had poor working conditions, low wages, child labour and 18-hour workdays. By 1839, thousands of children worked in Manchester cotton mills, only to be banned during the middle of the 19th century.

Children were particularly useful in the newly mechanised mills and factories, their small hands were used to fix broken threads on weaving and spinning machines across Europe and USA.

---

33. Kassia St Clair, The Golden Thread, How fabric changed history. Pg. 170

34. Arthur Haberman, The Making of the Modern Age. (Toronto: Gage Publishing, 1984)

With the arrival of these inventions, the cost of making cotton yarn dropped. By 1812, it was down by nine-tenths and the number of workers needed to turn wool into yarn had been reduced by four-f ifths.[35]

The addition of these inventions to the work force moved the stress from production to the supply of raw cotton. Within just a 35-year period, more than 100,000 power looms with 9,330,000 spindles were put into service in England and Scotland.[36]

Britain took advantage of the Americas' available new cotton, using it to help absorb demand. By 1830, the importation of raw cotton had increased to eight times its past rate and half of Britain's exports were refined cotton. All these evolutions created lead way for the steam engine, to power up these new machines.

More and more British workers moved from the countryside to the cities, creating an agricultural shortage. Six of every seven English workers were employed outside agriculture by 1870, and they needed to be fed, cheaply, and American agriculture was prepared to do exactly that.[37] By 1870, a quarter of American machine production was devoted to farm machinery.[38] To cheaper operate the land, producing more food and fibre to feed the machines and workers pushed the industrial revolution.

---

35. Gerhard Rempel. The Industrial Revolution. (Feb. 8, 2003)

36. Steve Kreis, Lecture 17: The Origins of the Industrial Revolution in England. In The History Guide, (Feb. 1, 2003)

37. Raj Patel and Jason W Moore, History of the Wold in Seven Cheap Things: A Guide to Capitalism, Nature and the Future of the Planet. Pg. 103 – 110

38. Brian Page and Richard Walker, From Settlement to Fordism: The agro-industrial revolution of the American Midwest. In Economic Geography, Vol. 67, No. 4 (Okt, 1991) (281 – 315) Pg. 308

Fashion and textile calls people to cities

Fashion and urbanisation have got a very strong historic connection, responsible as they are for some of the biggest migrations in history.

Over 100 years ago, 80% of humanity was living in rural environments. Now, over 50% of the world's population lives in an urban environment. And it's estimated that within the next 50 years, up to 75% of the world's population will live in a city.[39]

This can be good or bad. Potentially, it means that we've got greater opportunities for efficiency and connection. And yet at the moment, urban environments are places where social inequality is at its worst. Levels of poverty, of destitution, and disconnection between people occur within our urban environments. In the main textile-making countries, people are moving to the cities every day, young, unskilled workers that easily fall victim to the exploitation of the textile manufacturing units.

The constant supply of new workers makes it easier for companies to maintain a hostile workplace. If workers complain, they are simply replaced by the new arrivals. Textile and garment factories take advantage of a wide pool of young women, migrating from the poor rural areas into the city.[40]

Throughout the Industrial Revolution, for the first time, textile production was no longer a job for homeworkers and hands but took place in factories and by machines.

---

39. United Nations, World population prospects 2022, summary of results. (New York: United Nations, 2022) Projected is that by 2050, the world population will have reached 9.7 billion.

40. Out of 180 workers in Bangladesh, interviewed for the Microfinance Opportunities/Fashion Revolution Garment Worker Diaries project in 2017, 60% reported gender-based discrimination, over 15% reported being threatened and 5% had been hit. Fashion Revolution, Garment Worker Diaries. (London: Fashion Revolution, 2018)

Still, even at the height of the Industrial Revolution, the British output was peanuts on a global scale. Chinese spinners and weavers were producing 420 times as much cotton as their British counterparts were making in 1800.

While Indian spinners needed 50,000 hours to spin 100 pounds into yarn by hand, a Crompton's mule could accomplish the same task in a fiftieth of the time.[41] Due to the sheer volume Britain was able to produce, their price of yarn and cloth drastically decreased, making it highly competitive on the international market.

In 1830 a pound of British No. 40 yarn, a fine grade of thread, was three times cheaper than its Indian counterpart, eventually leading to subcontinental weavers purchasing cheap English thread reimported to India.[42]

Prior to the Industrial revolution, cotton was a side crop, grown by farmers alongside food. To supply to the large-scale demand of fibre-hungry factories, bigger specialised farms dedicated to fibre supply became the norm to create a steady supply of raw resources to process. American cotton farms in particular were happy to provide this, focusing on monocrop cotton farming. In the late 17th century India accounted for 95 per cent of the British import but by the late 1850s nearly 80 % of cotton consumed in Britain came from America.

To cater to the ever-growing demand in the US improvements were made to optimise the growth of cotton fibres, by looking for the cotton variety that would give the biggest yield, by improving the ginning process and exorbitantly increasing the farmland.

Eli Whitney created a new type of gin, able to comb out the seeds without breaking the cotton fibres, increasing the volume one person could clean by hand dramatically. The increase of cotton output of

41. Kassia St Clair, The Golden Thread, How fabric changed history. Pg 170

42. Steve Beckert, Empire of Cotton: A Global History. (New York: Vintage, 2015) Pg. 66-67, 80

South Carolina was staggering: in 1790 about 10,000 pounds of cotton was exported, by 1800 this increased to 6.4 million pounds.

The new, faster ginning process logically demanded more cotton plantations, more slaves and poor, working-class migrant workers to be put to work. Slaves were soon outnumbering the free inhabitants in most Southern states.[43]

The reign of cheap American cotton was abruptly halted by the entry of the boweevil in 1892, cotton-infesting insects that destroyed crops for the better part of the 20th century. This created a shift in main sourcing geography. Focus went back to China and India, complimented by Pakistan, Brazil, Indonesia, Turkey, and the United States. We still see the majority of our fibres come from these places today.[44]

Rise of the workforce

The cotton industry was the site of some of the earliest workers' strikes on both sides of the Atlantic. In *Empire of Cotton*, Sven Beckert reports cotton workers protesting in Britain in 1792 and handloom weaver petitions for a minimum wage in 1807 supported by 130,000 signatures[45]. The first US strike was led by women in 1824, when they walked away from a Rhode Island cotton mill. It is no coincidence that at the other end of the industry, in the fields from which its raw materials were extracted, slaves rebelled. Again, this was a global phenomenon happening across industries, on cotton and sugar

---

43. By 1860 the fifteen Southern states had 819,000 white male farmers, set against a slave population of 3.2 million. Slaves made up 50 per cent of the population in the main cotton states. Kassia St Clair, The Golden Thread, How fabric changed history. Pg 173

44. Due to the economic importance of cotton, the World Trade Organization holds a world cotton day each year, disclosing data about the current production patterns.

45. Steve Beckert, Empire of Cotton: A Global History. Pg 194

plantations everywhere form the United States through Martinique to Bahia, Brazil, which saw a Muslim slave uprising in 1835.

The exhaustion of the land called for the push of frontiers. New territories needed to be found to be exploited. And we still operate like this today. We push borders every day when we claim a new part of the rainforest to grow cattle and livestock feed. Humans have for centuries simply appropriated more, to enable our consumption habits to expand. We never reconsidered if we had enough, or even too much. Or whether we should optimise our yield to be able to make do with what we had. We just claimed more. More cheap labour in the form of slaves imported, more cheap land by cutting down forests and reclaiming it for the agro industry.

Educated workers are empowered workers

Given the scale and power of the textile industry, there are two possible approaches to improving the living situation of workers.

On an international level new boundaries need to be set, with regards to acceptable practices. History has shown us that, if a country changes policy, and worker rights are achieved, salaries rise, creating better living circumstances for workers. But history unfortunately also shows that when new laws demanding safer work environment and more realistic salaries come into effect, big companies leave the country looking for a poorer, more defenceless place to exploit. So, laws only really work, within an international framework.

Another option is to start from the ground up, improving the vocality of the workers, giving them a seat at the negotiation table in the form of a union. This is parallel to brands becoming fully transparent about their manufacturing situations and locations.

The garment industry is characterised by very low-rate unionisation – between 2 and 5 % depending on the source.[46]

Many of the people who make our clothes work in dirty, dangerous, and exhausting conditions. To address these conditions, a union remains the main direct tool for workers to establish their fundamental rights and improve their benefits. And if there is a CBA, a Collective Bargaining Agreement, which is legal binding and legally allows workers access to more benefits, their lives can improve beyond labour laws. It has the capacity to enhance the safety, health, and welfare of the people at work.

Whenever you have an independent, democratic and functioning union in a factory, that union will try to work with management for example to improve and reduce working hours, bargaining with management to get additional money for higher wages, or perhaps a bonus. Unions if they seek to bargain with management can also deal with very concrete and practical issues. Think about things like adequate and clean toilets, quality of food in the canteen or the question if the chair in which they're sitting for 10 hours a day is comfortable and ergonomic.[47]

NGOs like the Clean Clothing Campaign educate workers about their rights and responsibility, all related to labour laws, leadership negotiations, conflict, occupational health and safety[48], nutrition, sanitation, drinking water, and much more. They help create committees within factories to fight against gender-based violence, and for the implementation of anti-harassment rules.

---

46. Clean Clothing Campaign, Made by Women. Gender, The global garment industry and the movement for women workers' rights. (Clean Clothes Campaign, 2005)

47. Clean Clothing Campaign, Made by Women. Gender, The global garment industry and the movement for women workers' rights. (Clean Clothes Campaign, 2005)

48. This includes topics like maternal health, reproductive rights, HIV, AIDS, STDs, and much more including child growth.

One of the big reasons for the low unionisation rate is that unions are great for workers, but factory managers want to avoid them at all costs. The moment you do have workers join or form a union of their own choosing or basically seeking support with each other and building power together, that's the moment when workers are also going to ask for things that improve their lives, like higher wages or safer buildings or shorter working hours and so forth. All things that cost money and that are eating away the profit margin of either the factory or the brand. Factory managers are under constant pressure from brands to produce more cheaply. The threat of being replaced by a cheaper factory, in a less regulated country is constant.

Given that it's the brand who has the power in the relationship, any improvement to the work conditions is basically going to eat away the profits of the factory. Factory managers hesitate to agree to any increase in wages or improve their working situation in fear of losing competitive advantage and losing the brand orders.

Homeworking

Another way factories, factory managers and brands keep union at bay is by relying heavily on homeworkers.

Homeworking is very common across supply chains in the fashion industry. Homeworking entails people who are subcontracted, working from home, and commonly paid per piece they produce rather than an hourly wage. They often work without formal contracts or insurance and are paid in cash.

Homeworkers are mostly female and because they are part of the informal economy, they do not have the same legal protection as formal workers. If they face exploitation, it is difficult for them to seek recourse. This is true not just for cheap clothing but also in the luxury fashion sector. An investigation by the New York Times found unregulated homeworkers in parts of Italy getting paid €1.50

to €2.00 per hour and working 16 to 18 hours per day to make luxury garments for big name brands[49].

Privileged hierarchy of work

Within the textile industry we can distinguish different layers of work.

Certain types of work are more commonly performed in certain types of income level countries, because of the global value we have attributed to it. When I say global value it means the price we are willing to pay today for this service or product. If we don't value the work highly, we are not willing to pay a decent price for it, we ask low- or medium-income communities to do the job, since high income communities are not willing to pay the actual time the product took, at a full high income country salary.

Today the push to get clothes cheaper, faster and in ever-growing quantities is omnipresent. Factories make a habit of putting pressure on their workers, subjecting them to harassment, coercion, intimidation, and violence along the way.

Human hands make all cloth

The real price of any garment should be calculated using wages for the farmer, the ginner, the spinner, the whole supply chain.

And that is a price nobody wants to pay for a garment.

Small brands that are making the garments in-house, showing transparency for the product, and asking a fair price find themselves defending their prices. And this is still not considering the fact that their materials are often not made in fairly paid conditions.

---

49. Elizabeth Paton and Milena Lazazzera, Inside Italy's Shadow Economy. In New York Times, (Sept. 20, 2019)

In my company we have started from the beginning with organic materials, certified factories with unions and visiting all tiers of our production. We are by no means perfect, and we learn every season. Our prices represent the fair prices we pay at every level. Every sale we make, we need to defend our price build up. The transparency we offer helps customers understand. After nine years, I still regularly wonder about the living situations and payments that our fibre producers receive. It is a very hard thing to figure out since most is obscured by company trade secrets. We might know from which country our fibres come but pinpointing an actual farm has proven very challenging. I have experienced first-hand how the public perceives our prices as expensive, while what these prices actually just represent is a fair cost to all who assemble our clothes. As far as we know, all the people making our fibres and textiles are also paid fairly, but this is something that after nine years of research, I'm still not entirely sure of or have solid proof of.

People often ask why linen is such an expensive material. The main reason is that it is made in Europe, under European labour laws. Thus, the cost of processing is at a completely different level than in India or China, even though these materials often travel to those countries to be turned into yarn, or dyed, or woven. And China has a big linen industry as well, profiting from the price set by the European producers.

Yes, living costs are very different from one country to another. But when even a holiday in their own country is unaffordable on their salary, and we love backpacking around their country wearing what they produced, what kind of fair practice is that? The inequality is so embedded in our thinking that it is very hard to image life differently.

But we must.

Exploitation has no limits

For the last 20 years I have been listening to stories of my students while teaching in schools throughout Europe. Each school agrees that internships are the ideal way for students to really understand the requirements, the pace and learn the ways of the world. And students would come back from their internship with much fewer illusions about fashion, but also with stories of exploitation, companies making them perform two days of testing, basically sewing pieces for the company's production, to be judged based on that. And if they were "chosen" they would spend the next six months in a foreign country, with no salary, working easily 10 hours a day sewing pieces together for testing, for celebrities, for fashion shows. With the "great" opportunity that they could observe the designer at work, as long as they did not talk, interfere or in any way annoyed the creative head of the studio.

Understanding the educational part of these experiences has become hard. And these kinds of exploitative internships are so common; I've heard many first-hand accounts of companies in Amsterdam, London, New York, Mumbai. France is today a solitary exception. In France interns are put to work, and are not supposed to be heard or seen, and for the first six weeks are not paid. But after that, companies are required by law to provide a minimum salary, giving the interns rights, protection of the law and making the general operation much more equal.

I think that fashion professionals need to be curious and willing to learn and look outside their usual roles in order to think about what solutions they can come up with and how they can help to move things forward in a really positive way.

If you design and make garments for shows, and celebrities, costing fortunes, but these garments are fully produced by as many as 20 interns "learning" in your office for six months, how is this any different from working with slaves? Is it justifiable because they choose to be there? They have no real choice. Schools consider internships an integral part of their curriculum, and after graduation, many graduates still spend one to two years doing free internships in the hope of eventually being offered an entry level job.

Because of the imbalance of companies relying heavily on unpaid labour, prices of designer pieces are often very arbitrary.

The idea to no longer only discuss minimum wage vs living wage, but to create the openness to discuss the lowest pay grade in the chain might be shocking to many. If one flips the pages of any high-end fashion magazine, the amount of free labour, the result of exploited workers is outrageous, produced in all countries around the world.

Starting my career working for a designer, I had a wakeup call when confronted with the ambiguous relation fashion has with its petit mains, the makers. In couture houses they are revered; in fast fashion they are hidden out of sight. But they always remain merely the executors of ideas developed somewhere higher up the chain of command who control their quality of life.

SOCIAL FOUNDATION, BASIC HUMAN NEEDS

Just Change

Space is such a lovely word. Its undefined, yet we all have an intuitive understanding of what it means. In history we have approached the word either as an absolute or a relative term. The origin for this dichotomy are the contradicting opinions of the Greeks Aristotle and Plato.

Plato defined space as absolute: for him objects in a room are irrelevant to the space. Space is absolute, not interfered by the object that moves within it. Space has no qualities of its own[50] : it is a pure medium within which objects exist and processes take place. This concept of space when applied to a theatre set, means space will not change, even if the actors move, have different roles, walk in and around the furniture on stage.

Aristotle had a different approach: he defined space as the relation between objects. This is a relative definition. When the object in a room moves, the space is reconfigured and thus changes. This view holds space as an extendable limit, described as: "the limit of the surrounding body, at which it is in contact with that which is surrounded [i.e., the thing]" [51] Space is an envelope that surrounds a thing, and it changes, grows, and is destroyed with the thing.

Applied to the same example, the set, actors, their roles, and texts actually make the space. If anything in the setting moves or is altered, then the space is changed.

When we talk about space in terms of this philosophical debate, it discusses the problem of permanence and change, or the relation between being and becoming. It investigates the ideas of reality and appearance. The opposition highlights the fundamental conflict of what could be approached by reason and what is met by the senses.

---

50. Plato, Timaeus, 50e

51. Artistotle Physics, 209b 5-6

The fashion industry has a form of being, and simultaneously is constantly reinventing itself.

Fashion appeals to the senses, but if we want to talk about the sustainable practices it could entail, this calls upon our reason.

It might feel like things have been done in set ways for so long that change is beyond reach. By questioning the difference between what fashion is, and what it could become, ideals become valid goals. We need to have knowledge and a deep understanding of the universal essential features of the fashion industry to keep the good and modify what is causing harm.

From that point, I believe the idea of space in Aristotle's view is much more beneficial than Plato's. If we see the space fashion occupies as something that is constructed by all its elements, then any change we make to the players and the elements will change the fashion space itself.

If you want to understand how change is possible, even in the simplest sense of movement from one place to another, you need an account of the space across which that thing moves. Even though everyone agrees that space has some sort of existence, Aristotle tells us, it is not an easy thing to say exactly what it is.[52]

Accept that we are just reconfiguring our global space.

---

52. Artistotle Physics, 209b 20-33

Exploitation today

In the light of history, it is no surprise that women, children and the poorest in society are still being exploited in the textile industry today.

Predictably, modern day slavery is still found, in the form of forced labour. And, sadly, child labour is still present in many textile countries. Legally it is abolished, but practically it can still be easily found. Most of the 24 biggest brands in the world cannot say for certain no children or slaves have worked on their garments.

The textile industry has profited of them since its very origin.

Each generation has identified a suffering we no longer stand with. Slavery was officially abolished in 1926, the Universal Declaration of Human rights and Equality came into effect in 1947 and child labour was condemned internationally in 1990 with legislation intended to terminate it. The same condemnation is happening for animal cruelty and speciisme today.

So, our global space is changing.

Many things contribute to the status quo of today. But as a designer and as a brand, an enormous power lies within your reach.

- Within your company, ensure equal pay for equal jobs.

- Make sure everyone has the same opportunities to promotions. Create a safe work environment for all.

- Demand to be transparent. Not only internally in your company, but also externally to your suppliers and consumers, communicate about it. Advocate for full transparency.

- Demand to produce in factories that have unions.

- Implement female teaching programs, with positive discrimination when time for promotions comes around in your company and demand it in the companies that you work with.

- Investigate all tiers of your supply chain, don't stop at the manufacturing level, look beyond, to the farm, the fibre-making, the fabric making.

- Pay a living wage, not a minimum wage and demand the same of your contractors and subcontractors. Know what the living wage is, in the countries and districts you work with. And evaluate this regularly. Life gets more expensive everywhere.

- Talk to the workers on the work floor. Visit and invest in the people that realise the dreams. But be conscious that your visit will remain incomplete and coloured. After all, you are the foreigner or stranger visiting.

- Don't rely on only auditing, your visits, or the demands made by certain labels like GOTS or Fair Trade, perform your own. And dare to look at the results. Companies like &Wider are using social audits to uncover the real sensitive date, so brands know the real situation and act accordingly.[53]

- Take positive action to reduce gender-based discrimination, exploitation and violence towards all people working across your value chain.

- Make sure your company has a global policy, it is a global industry after all.

---

53. &Wider is a great company that developed data driven tools to directly, anonymously gather information from the people making the goods. By means of automated calls that are mobile friendly, workers can express grievances, incident reporting and give a real insight in their work situation. Allowing brands to act accordingly, implement improvement policies and follow up on progress and identify priorities.

Human suffering in the textile industry is hidden within many corners and shadows. From children living in villages where groundwater is completely polluted to farmers risking their lives due to the pesticides they feel obliged to use on their crops, to the dyeing of textile and much more. There are workers forced to leave their children behind in villages, working too many hours for too little money in buildings that are not safe, with no protection against exploitation or sexual, physical, or psychological abuse.

The people working in the shops,[54] selling fast fashion, with too little social security, and salary, with no long-term contracts available.

And all the way up to the design houses with interns who are not paid, but whom companies depend on for making part of the production.

Due to the complex nature of fashion supply chains, it can be difficult for a brand to identify where women are harassed and intimidated in their supply chain. For brands to ensure that there aren't children working in the production of their goods, it is important for them to map their suppliers all the way down to the raw material.

It isn't enough for a brand to know the factory where their shirts are made, they need to trace the product from farm to fibre to textile to finished garment. Child labour tends to occur most frequently at earlier stages of production on farms and in textile mills. Modern slavery is always hidden somewhere under disguise of a subcontractor. Women are withheld a voice by their male bosses.

Nothing is free, nothing is cheap. So, somebody is always paying. Who are they? They are the workers, they're the females, they are the

---

54. According to Trade Union Congress, retail is the worst industry in the UK for pay and progression, with just over half a million workers aged between 18 and 29 stuck in low-paid retail work. Arthur Harrop, Thousands of low-paid retail workers are getting stuck, not getting on. (London: Trade Union Congress, May 3, 2018)

SPACE, A SOCIAL ENVIRONMENT   113

young, the children who are producing the most sold commodities: clothing.

The greatest barrier to ending modern slavery is obscurity of the supply chain.

The biggest help in fighting child labour in a supply chain is traceability.

The greatest impact on female work safety is increasing transparency.

And paying all a living wage.

That's plain decency and the first step to fundamentally changing our global public space.

> "To protect our natural world, (our humanity and the natural resources of our earth,) we need to participate in the fight for justice for all people and leave no one behind."[55]

---

55. Greenpeace International July 11, 2020 instagram

Seven

Mending fashion's economic model

T HIS CHAPTER IS DEDICATED to designing value, redesigning economic thinking and the economic implications if one decides to set up a positive company.

The first questions any investor or bank asks today are: what is the economic relevance of what you wish to achieve, and how are you going to create growth and profit?

So, in that line of thinking, if we want to make our fashion industry sustainable, it also needs to be financially self-sufficient.

For me as an entrepreneur, it makes no sense to invent and experiment with business processes that are only functional within a sponsored, government-financed climate. The question is how to establish ongoing structural change.

Communities and companies must feel in control of their own destinies and have the freedom to decide how to realize them. This brings a sense of community and shared responsibility.

A sustainable practice should be built to be self-sustaining, not dependent on external forces keeping it afloat. During the start-up phase, sponsorship, aid, or tax relief might be beneficiary, but in the long run, each project can only be called truly sustainable if it is also financially independent thus sustaining itself. To achieve fundamental change, any company moving to become a sustainable positive impact company, must create ways to allow this to happen, without relying on continual aid.

The reason I stress this from the start, is that in many countries and economies, aid has been so structurally embedded that we no longer even know it is there. The agricultural industry in Europe is a great example. It receives hundreds of millions of euros in aid every year, to keep farmers in business. Never is this questioned, even if the market prices are simply too low. The amount of food wasted each year in Europe is estimated to be at least 10% of food production, but is probably higher. Yet, Europeans are not motivated to create less waste, because we are not confronted with the actual price of our food. It is shielded from the public eye by governments that are not transparent and opaque EU funding.[1]

Taxpayers' money used to subsidize old fashioned business models, with little regard for changing demands or insights gained, is wasted money. For example, the European dairy industry keeps its dairy prices low, under pressure from big supermarkets, while their products are challenged by non-supported suppliers of plant-based alternatives. The actual price of milk is much higher, paid for by our collective taxes. One could easily argue that plant-based alternatives arrive at the market at competitive prices, with no government aid, and are ecologically more sensible. From an economic, ecologic, and human health perspective, this subsidy is questionable, and it enables needless animal cruelty. So why is the public's tax money sustaining this outdated agricultural model? Why not make those who love their milk, pay the actual costs instead of an artificially cheaper price?

For too long, funding and tax relief have provided aid without systemic support leading to situations where, if the aid stops, the systems collide and disappear, returning the community or industry to where they were before aid arrived, in need of financial help. Operations relying on external funding desperately need structural systemic change.

---

1. https://ec.europa.eu/food/safety/food_waste/eu-food-loss-waste-prevention-hub/resources
https://www.fi-compass.eu/funds/eafrd

Positive business

Our current economic logic is not delivering sustainability. The basic human needs of billions of people are not being met. Planetary boundaries are constantly pushed to the point where today we have surpassed many boundaries, leading to catastrophic climate change and biodiversity loss. Capitalism governs how we transform resources – such as cotton or oil or labour – into the things that we use in our lives every day – like clothing.[2] But the systems we employ to realize this transformation are completely up to us.

Given that at its core every company wants to survive, to still be here tomorrow, it makes economic sense to preserve our planet. Existing companies are realising this need and starting to understand their vital role in this. A sustainable policy is not a feel-good, nice-to-have policy. It is smart business, strengthening economic position and customer relationships. The change starts from within, driven by ethics, a desire for self-preservation and economic interests but it is gradual, and it will prove impossible to get back within the planetary boundaries with only this kind of change.

More radical change can be expected from the disruptive newcomers, those not hindered by the big, slow-functioning decision-making processes of big companies, or the prevailing traditions of doing things a certain way. A fresh start is needed exploring paths that will look very different than those to which we have grown accustomed. Fighting an existing reality is hard; building a new model, that makes the existing model obsolete[3] is one way of debunking old models that no longer serve our changed reality.

---

2. Simon Mair, Centre for Sustainable fashion Factsheet, Agenda. (London: University of the Arts London, 2018)

3. Paraphrasing Buckminster Fuller. Learning Journey, Circular Design.

Policymakers concern themselves with their public and try to please them by attempting to improve the economy. The environment is never given centre stage as it is too often regarded as something outside or apart from us humans.

But humans, society and the environment are interconnected, with the economy dependent on society and the environment while human existence and society are dependent on, and within the environment.[4]

The question is how to motivate companies to embrace sustainability in their core practice, especially given that such measures usually lead to escalating costs, at least during transition?[5] Governments can give endorsements, tax benefits or regulatory support. Citizens can show their appreciation by supporting companies that show transparency and effort while exploring the shifting sands of what is considered green.

Doughnut economies[6]

At the core of the desire to redefine a new sustainable economic system, lie two ground principles: firstly, that the planet we live on is limited and best visualized by the planetary boundaries; and sec-

---

4. Bob Giddings, Bill Hopwood and Geaff O'Brian, Environmnent, economy and society: Fitting them together into sustainable development. In Sustainable Development, Vol. 10 No. 4. pg 178-196 (n.d. John Wiley & Sons, Nov. 2002)

5. Paul Lanoie and George A. Tanguay, Factors Leading to Green Profitability. 10 case studies. In Greener Management International, Vol. 31, No. 3. (2000) pg. 39-50.

6. The term is the core of the theory defined by Kate Raworth. For those of you wanting further information on the implications of sustainable economics for the 21st century. Kate Raworth, Doughnut Economics: Seven Ways to Think like a 21st-Century Economist (London: Random House Business, 2018)

ondly that the social impact of economy needs to benefit all people on this planet, not just the lucky few.

Today the world's richest 1% own more wealth than all other 99% put together.[7] Human activity is putting unprecedented stress on Earth's life-giving systems.

Kate Raworth has developed a great model that shows where a safe human, ecologic and economic space for living in harmony is situated.

The model starts with introducing the outer boundaries of any safe space, illustrated as the outline of a doughnut. This outer boundary is the ecological ceiling of what is essential to maintain life on Earth. The inner boundary is made up of the essential social foundation for the well-being of all humankind.

To arrive within the safe boarders of this doughnut, economics must be redesigned to be distributive of the value it generates and re-generative to ensure Earth's and human's cyclical processes of life. Humanity's resources will need to be equitably distributed, to benefit all.

The doughnut is representative of the safe space that enables humanity to tackle and fundamentally change the problems as outlined in the two previous Chapters. And within the safe space of the dough-nut, an endless cradle-to-cradle loop of materials should flow to keep us in the doughnut and not start transgressing it again.

Scientists suggest that, if undisturbed, the Holocene's benevolent conditions for this planet would likely continue for another 50,000

7. Deborah Hardoon, Sophia Ayele and Ricardo Fuentes-Nieva, An economy for the 1%: how privileged and power in the economy drive extreme inequality and how this can be stopped. (Oxfam International, 2016)

years, due to the Earth's unusually circular orbit around the sun.[8] This projection holds tremendously positive information: if we find ways to halt our excess, our future will look bright. Living conditions as we have known it on earth would continue if we can halt human interference.

Today is an extraordinary moment in history. We are the first generation to understand properly the damage we have been doing to our planetary household, and probably the last generation with the chance to do something transformative about it.[9] If we master the key to entering the doughnut sphere, we will have found a way to live within the human-dominated Anthropocene, while maintaining the ecological equilibrium of the Holocene, where humans have been thriving in for almost the entire history of humanity.[10]

Facing our globally connected economy and fashion industry will require collaboration, accountability, and experimentation to find the working keys for this new reality. Human existence is limited by the planet we live on and thus our businesses should reflect this reality. There is only so much at our disposal: if we use more of the planet's resources, others will have less; and if we use more than our Earth can regenerate then we destroy the Earth altogether.

---

8. A. Berger and M. Loutre, An Exceptionally Long Interglacial Ahead? In Science, Vol. 297, issue 5585. (August 23, 2002) pg 1287 – 1288

9. Kate Raworth, Doughnut Economics: Seven Ways to Think like a 21st-Century Economist. pg. 286

10. It started approx. 11,700 years ago.

DOUGHNUT ECONOMICS

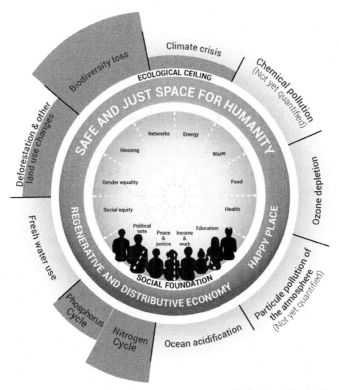

After Kate Raworth, Doughnut Economics

The economy is an open system with constant inflows and outflows of matter and energy. It depends on the Earth as a source, and likewise as a sink for its wastes. Earth itself, however, is a closed system because almost no matter leaves or arrives on this planet: energy from the sun may flow through it, but materials can only cycle within it.[11]

For a healthier, happier existence radical change must be realised for humanity and the planet in terms of political structures, government taxes and encouragement, and redefining economic fields.

---

11. Herman E. Daly and Joshua Farley. Ecological economics: principles and applications. (Washington, Island Press, 2011) pg. 16

Many ecological economists like Raworth and Kallis[12] are working on the development of new ideas and systems. While this approach to economics is young, it is my hope that many of the changes suggested will become mainstream and implemented soon.

The state has a responsibility to provide public goods and services, but it is not the clean, positive good services and goods that we, the community the state is supposed to serve, are paying for via our taxes. Governments have the power to create regulations that promote and support common goals, creating frameworks within which positive actions are rewarded, and negative, destructive, and polluting industries are penalized.

In order not to lose focus on our direction, we will mostly be looking at how companies, especially fashion companies can structure themselves against a new reality that holds new demands and challenges. How do we create a self-sustaining community of people in different countries, working towards a mutual goal?

In general, the economics of clothing involves several processes: material extraction, production, distribution, consumption, and disposal. These processes are interrelated and inseparable. Yet the last phase – disposal – as an economical opportunity, has not been explored much. The whole system today is fiercely competitive and obsessed with growth.

The old-fashioned linear model

A linear 'take, make, dispose' mentality is advocated by the current leading economic model which systemically undervalues nature and the underlying principles of humanity. It relies on large quantities of cheap, easily accessible materials and energy, has been at the heart

---

12. Giorgos Kallis, Giacomo D'Alisa and Federico Demaria (ed.) , Degrowth, A Vocabulary for a New Era. (New York: Routledge, 2015)

of industrial development and has generated an unprecedented level of growth.

The model considers the Earth's resources as an endless flow of materials taking them as needed, with no consideration about how much is right, or just, or equal, or even how much can be used before it starts depleting and destroying our ecosystem. The premise of all those cheap resources has in fact been catastrophically expensive: it makes goods, intended to be consumed.

Between 2000 and 2015, the number of garments produced annually doubled. The annual number of garments produced exceeded 100 billion for the first time in 2014. That is nearly 14 items of clothing for every person on Earth.

With the increase of production, streamlined operations and pushing costs, brands were able to maintain their sales prices, while consumer spending budgets have steadily risen in the past 50 years, creating ever increasing sales.

Sales have been robust around the globe, but most notably, it is emerging economies that have seen an exceptionally large rise in clothing sales, as their peoples have joined the middle class.[13] The impact of this increase in the global consumer market will be enormous over the next few years.

---

13. In five large developing countries—Brazil, China, India, Mexico, and Russia—apparel sales grew eight times faster than in Canada, Germany, the United Kingdom, and the United States. But, even after this increase, the average developing-country resident purchases a fraction of the clothing that his or her developed-world counterpart buys each year. Overall clothing sales will rise significantly when developing-country consumers start to buy more clothing due to their increase in purchasing power. The middle class is on the rise in emerging economies worldwide, and this will dramatically influence the consumption amounts of garments worldwide.

In the first world there has also been a steady increase of sales. The idea that one day we will have enough, or the idea that we still need as many pieces today as we needed 10 years ago is non-existent. We only have one body – yet the amount we purchase annually keeps increasing.

It mostly has to do with the mindset that we don't buy to possess, we buy to use, and use up: buying, wearing for a short time, and then discarding. The inherent value of our purchases seems to be near to nothing: certain reports indicate that the average garment is worn just seven or eight times before being disposed of.

The consumer goods industry has done a stellar job in convincing consumers that the value of an item is a combination of the social status it will give you, and a devaluation of the hard work, energy, and material used to create it. Basically, devaluing the goods themselves and turning them into disposables.

The consumer goods mindset teaches people that the value of every purchased good is almost nothing. So why cherish your garments, care for them, or mend them?

When price is the major point of competition between companies, margins are squeezed at every stage to maximize profit, the question of sustainability is a costly additional feature, and one of the first in budget cuts.[14]

Consumption, overconsumption, and self-worth

The origins of the term 'consumption' are found in the act of wasting, of destroying the object by its use: when one consumes an apple, it will be destroyed by the act of eating it, consuming it.

How did we get to a point where we believe that we can consume things like cars, garments, and mobile phones?

---

14. Sophie Buchel et al. The transition to good fashion. DRIFT report. (Rotterdam, Erasmus University Rotterdam, 2018)

People learned that consumer goods are an expression of status, and that they can be accumulated. And this is linked to the created idea of scarcity: the fear that there will not be enough resources (limited edition bags, special model cars, etc.) will motivate purchases.

Brands are all too aware of this mechanism, so a false sense of scarcity is constantly created to encourage people to consume more. The belief that there will never be enough causes fear, stress, and anxiety. This is heavily fuelled by our online presence. Online we are confronted with an endless flow of things we don't have, things we don't do, places we don't visit, and the illusion that everyone else around us is living a much more abundant life than we are.

The endless flow of images of things and events we are missing out on, resulting in FOMO, Fear Of Missing Out. It emphasizes that we need to own more, buy more, and every season there is a steady flow of new things to possess. We are made hyperaware of all we lack. Only when we reduce our online presence, stop comparing ourselves to others and become content with what we have and do, can these feelings subside.

Simply thinking like a consumer our sense of community and, unlike the engaged citizens we should be, we no longer act from shared values.[15]

15. Kate Raworth, Doughnut Economics: Seven Ways to Think like a 21st-Century Economist. pg. 121

The irony of this is inescapable: a false sense of scarcity is created to make us feel unsafe, and that in turn makes us consume even more – and this is what fuels an actual scarcity.[16]

This linear model has enabled businesses to aggressively streamline their supply chains and cut costs causing the price of clothing to fall relative to the prices of other consumer goods. Is it good business to optimize the costs and increase the retail price as much as the fake scarcity allowed?

Pressure from multiple angles

NGO's have been working relentlessly to push back consumerism in favour of engaged thinking. Awareness about the social impact of our value chain has risen due to high-profile social incidents like the Rana Plaza disaster in 2013, in which over 1,000 workers were killed. Greenpeace's Detox campaign shed light on the specific challenges of chemical misuse, dyeing waterways in next year's fashion colours. Fashion Revolution has created campaigns to drive awareness of the way clothes are made. Each campaign highlights elements that make business as usual sound illogical.

---

16. Sometimes even the impression of scarcity is enough. One example is "The Drop". By utilising social and digital media, an announcement is made about the release of a product, with short term notice. The hype is fuelled and cultivated by announcing the limited edition and exclusivity of said product. The release is either only at limited physical retail locations, or online locations for a very limited time. undefinedAnother technique is what H&M has been perfecting over the last 20 years by collaborating with upscale, highly sought-after designer brands to create a capsule, in limited models, limited stores, limited quantities – with heavy pre-launch advertising. Long queues before opening hours and in-store fights have become the new normal, following in similar vein to the launch of a new tech product like the new iPhone or PlayStation.

Fashion is unravelling at the seams. The wear and tear of the current model is becoming more and more apparent as people and planet are harmed in favour of economic gain. And we need to mend it, but possibly also tackle the unstable foundations.

The very context needed to enable a linear modus operandi is changing. Customers are becoming increasingly aware and critical about what kind of business they support with their purchase. The limitations of our Earth are clearer, showing material and energy scarcity. Unions are forming and demanding better social situations in the making processes, and governments are implementing stricter regulations at every turn. The whole operating system of taking, making, and disposing is being challenged and questioned.

Taking

Companies have noticed that a linear system leads to an increased exposure to risk; most notably from resource price fluctuations (cotton prices have been volatile since the beginning of the pandemic) and disruptions in the supply chain (strikes have lately been occurring in China, India and Bangladesh for various social mishaps).

To protect themselves against potentially higher costs, most companies have responded similarly, clinging to the old model, by beating down harder on the supply chain. During the outbreak of the pandemic many companies cut ties with their suppliers, left them with ordered produce, refusing to pay. Companies started renegotiating production prices long after purchase orders were issued, to push down risks and costs. The transactional relationships, fragmented, and unequal in their power, placed a disproportionate amount of social and environmental risk on the poorest and lowest in the chain. Farmers, makers, and suppliers suffered the hardest with the dramatic shift in demand during wave after wave of lockdowns.[17]

---

17. Sophie Buchel et al. The transition to good fashion. DRIFT report. (Rotterdam, Erasmus University Rotterdam, 2018)

Social media has led to a global outrage about this, fuelled by extensive reporting by NGOs worldwide, calling on brands to #Pay Up. It highlighted brands refusing to pay what they ordered, even if the goods were already in the harbour ready to be shipped. Giving the pandemic as the reason, companies were renegotiating prices and asking for 90% discount, without reasoning that a pandemic inherently means that the global economy is affected, and those working at the bottom of the supply chain suffer the most.

The horror stories were many: in Bangladesh people were fired and not paid; in the Philippines Covid was the excuse for firing them, which conveniently coincided with the establishment of a union; in India many factories have been stuck with merchandise ordered, made to measure, but not pick up or paid for. Their margins suddenly had to stretch to pay for their workers' safety and wellbeing while stuck in a government-enforced total lockdown for months. Till today those issues have not been resolved, the brands just moved country and supplier leaving their old suppliers in the cold.

Fashion as the big machine it is, also does not just reopen. As any factory manager knows, you don't just depend on your workers, but also on your supplies. If your suppliers also had to stop the machines, and the moving of raw materials fully halted, and fibres could no longer be collected from the fields and sold, then getting each part running again, is easier said than done. Shortages on the cotton market only started showing eight months after first lockdowns.

Most likely the fluctuations in rare material prices and agricultural crops supply will only increase due to further depletion of the resources and climate change making harvests hard to predict. But still this natural capital is consumed as a low-cost inflow.

Making

Another notable risk is the dependency on external supply. We are globally connected. A few areas of the world possess deposits of non-renewable resources, but most rely on imports. The European Union imports six times as many materials and natural resources as it exports.[18] A linear model is highly dependent on a steady flow of energy and raw materials. As we have seen, the political instability has caused huge price swings. Volatile climate situations like the flooding in Bangladesh in May 2022 only add further pressure on supply chains.

Disposing

In recent years there have been increased efforts by regulators to implement climate change laws and taxes.[19] Carbon tax and landfill tax are just two examples of ways the government tries to bring value back to our waste.

The linear fashion model is surprisingly wasteful in how it creates value, and which part of its value chain is considered valuable. Its waste has been neglected as economically worthy. In fashion we lose fibres during stages of spinning and weaving; and more significantly about 10-15% of fabric used is left behind on the cutting floor. We recycle about 1% of all garments produced. About 92 million tons

---

18. Frans Timmermans et al. Weg mit der Wegwerfmentalität. In Die Zeit (May 28, 2015)

19. GLOBE, M. Nachmany et al. The GLOBE Climate Legislation Study: A Review of Climate Change Legislation in 66 Countries. Fourth Edition. (London: GLOBE International and the Grantham Research Institute, London School of Economics, 2014) Between 2009 and 2014, the number of climate change laws has increased by 66%, from 300 to 500, in de 66 reviewed countries.

DESIGN FOR WASTE
Value chain

DESIGN

PRODUCTION

CONSUMPTION

WASTE

of garment-related waste is discarded every year. That is almost as much as it creates annually.[20]

The 3% conundrum

We live in a time where a 3% profit is regarded as normal. After reading about the topic, and upon lots of reflection, it left me puzzled. Human beings historically have an incredibly hard time understanding exponential growth. During the current pandemic the news was filled with reproduction numbers on how fast the virus was spreading, and the exponential growth of infections. Humans seem to lack an intuitive understanding of the implication of exponential growth.

As the story goes, when the game of chess was first presented to a great king, he offered the inventor any reward that he wanted. The inventor asked that a single grain of rice be placed on the first square of the chessboard. Then two grains on the second square, four grains on the third, and so on, doubling each time. The king, baffled by such a small price for a wonderful game, immediately concurred, and ordered the treasurer to pay the agreed upon sum. A week later, the inventor went before the king and asked why he had not received his reward. The king, outraged that the treasurer had disobeyed him, immediately summoned him, demanding to know why the inventor had not been paid. The treasurer explained that the sum could not be paid – by the time you got even halfway through the chessboard, the amount of grain required was more than the entire kingdom possessed. The king took in this information and thought for a while. Then he did the only rational thing a king could do in those circum-

---

20. Ellen MacArthur Foundation & McKinsey Center for Business and Environment. Growth within: A circular economy vision for a competitive Europe. (Jun 1, 2015) Chapter 1 for more detailed information on natural systems degradation. Our industry contributes to global environmental pressures including loss of biodiversity and natural capital, land degradation, ocean pollution, and in general by creating waste

stances: he had the inventor killed as an objective lesson in the perils of trying to outwit the king.[21]

The moral of the story is that pure exponential growth spirals out of control in a matter of moves or days. And even ruling kings can fail to grasp this sufficiently.

As this story shows, the idea of exponential growth is hard to intuitively predict. So, what does it say about our idea that the profit and growth of a company or of national growth can be maintained at 3%? If we believe that our economy, or the company profit will increase by 3% each year, that will mean we double our national economy, or the profit or our company every 23 years. It means that it would grow to more than 10 times its current size in about 80 years.

The more powerful question at hand is: growth of what, why, and for whom? Who will pay the cost, how long will it last and what will it cost our planet?[22] Blind growth is not qualitative per se, it is just a quantitative accumulation. The idea of limitless growth seems to act as a substitute for equality of income. We can accept destruction as a casualty along the way, as long as we have hope that one day, we will be on the top of the food chain. This hope is what makes large income differentials tolerable. We are willing to accept our situation, however miserable or unfair, in the hope that one day we will grow out of our situation.

But history has shown that growth of an economy or a company's profit does not necessarily influence or improve the poverty of its employees. Most of the biggest fashion companies still work with highly under-paid workers while their owners are featured in Forbes magazine's 100 Richest People list year after year.

---

21. Alex Knapp, The Seduction Of The Exponential Curve. In Forbes, (Nov. 17, 2011)

22. Kate Raworth, Doughnut Economics: Seven Ways to Think like a 21st-Century Economist, Donella Meadows, 1972 Limits to growth, pg. 40

To establish predicted growth, companies have an invested interest in keeping people in poverty and raw materials cheap. Pure growth does not entail an incentive to take better care of the planet or its workers. To expand and increase profits year on year makes most businesses fail in the context of planetary boundaries and human equality.

Sustainable prosperity in environmental, social, *and* financial terms will require a different thinking system and a new definition of growth. [23] It will also require us to think; when do we have enough?

We are WEIRD[24]

For the longest time, the western capitalistic approach to living together has been dominant. It's so ingrained in the culture I grew up in, that thinking about a different system is a challenge.

Growing up in Belgium, everybody always aimed at being able to buy a house as soon as possible. Having things relates to social status, and projects success. Everything can be bought or purchased for the right price. And we thrive on assets, possessing things.

Joseph Henrik developed a term, WEIRD, to describe this way of life: Western, Educated, Industrial, Rich, Democratic citizens and nations. In this way of life, capitalism thrives because with every purchase we make or get something and sell it for more money than it cost us. Capital needs to be accumulated.

---

23. Ellen MacArthur Foundation & McKinsey Center for Business and Environment. Growth within: A circular economy vision for a competitive Europe. (Jun 1, 2015)

24. Acronym used by anthropologist Joseph Henrich to argue that Westerners are the outliers. Kate Raworth, Doughnut Economics: Seven Ways to Think like a 21st-Century Economist pg. 282

Facing our current challenges, it will be especially the WEIRD that must change their aspirations and no longer only address growth as a synonym for the accumulation of things.

Growth might have been a driver for a long time, but if we change what drives us to something more social, engaged and connected, we might find a new definition for growth.

Generation Z has been pushing for radical change with many expressing their intuitive understanding that they will not be richer than their parents, that the future is more unreliable, and that they have little trust that they will live long enough to have big dreams or aspirations in our current approach to life. What a terrible feeling this must be. This generation understands that it is essential to generate other aspirations, meaningful goals, and ideals to live for, not just economic growth and retail therapy, and they are actively exploring other paths.

Thinking in what I now would define as old-fashioned systems, to grow, a company will use more materials to make more things and require more labour to realize those things. Both will simultaneously grow, with the growth of the profit and impact of your product.

Growth in this optic is not just about selling more stuff; it's also about reducing cost: i.e., selling the same amount of stuff but producing it more cheaply. This is what economists call productivity gains, and the problem with productivity gains is that they can degrade the production process.

Productivity gains often come through a combination of specialisation and mechanisation. And essentially this means, taking the craftsperson who is part of the process from design through manufacture and into delivery, and breaking it down into many small repetitive tasks that can be done either by unskilled workers or machinery. This has made production cheaper but resulted in the loss of craftsmanship. And the loss of craftsmanship can mean workers don't have creative input.[25]

Although in environmental terms we're getting more efficient at producing stuff, the overall impact of this production is growing because the total amount of stuff is growing. A t-shirt, or luxury item produced today might be more environmentally friendly than one produced 20 years ago, but we consume and produce an awful lot more of everything today, so the overall impact is still rising.

Naturally there is a side note; it might be that you can move your company away from needing more labour because you shift to using more automatized work by putting computers or robots to work. This however still leaves your company needing more and more materials.

All this demonstrates is that if you make products that do little damage, this is great compared to other polluting, non-conscious companies, or products, but in the long run, this small amount of pollution will grow explosively. And the negative impact will still be there and become bigger in time. Doing less damage is still not good enough in the long run.

Scientists have calculated that we have about a decade to make the necessary changes to avert catastrophic climate change. The much-needed shift in knowledge and behaviour is dramatic. Our current material use will need to be decreased by about 75 to 95 percent, compared to today's levels to return to the safe planetary boundaries. This requires quantitative reduction and much better qualitative use to enable endless reuse. And this quantitative reduction will be most felt by the Western, Educated, Industrial, Rich, Democratic citizens and nations.

Maybe instead of growth, we should think in terms of care. Care to maintain, continue, repair the world so that all can live in it as well

---

25. This is what that the art critic and political economist John Ruskin described as dehumanisation.

as possible[26] to rebuild the interwoven complex life-sustaining web that existence on Earth entails.

When you start, start positive

More and more nations have realized the impossibility of continuing business as usual. Attempts have been made on an international level to set standards and barriers in place, to reduce dependency on fossil fuels and to cut production of CO_2 emissions.[27] Government policies like eco-taxes can have an enormous positive impact. Germany raised the taxes on fossil fuels used for transport, heating and electricity while lowering payroll taxes by an equivalent amount between 1999 and 2003. As a result, the use of heavily taxed goods and commodities declined while services like car sharing rose. These types of policies create jobs and provide better quality of living with less environmental stress. Their impact however is not enough to bring us back within the doughnut's safe space.

We will need to fundamentally change on all levels if we want to return to liveable planetary boundaries. We have already transgressed some of the boundaries so enormously, that it will require more than good will and change from within.

So how do you start becoming a positive impact company? How can we consistently reduce our output, emissions, and reliance on limited resources? How can we move away from exploitation-reliant models of production and use of materials?

---

26. Maria Puig de la Bellacasa, Matters of Care: Speculative Ethics in More Than Human Worlds. (Minneapolis: University of Minnesota Press, 2017)

27. But as we have witnessed in countries like Germany, between 2000 and 2016 the Gross Domestic Product grew 16% while its consumption-based CO_2 emissions fell by 12%. Despite efforts to halt this, material uses still grew by 8% between 1990 and 2007. Kate Raworth, Doughnut Economics: Seven Ways to Think like a 21st-Century Economist. Pg 211-213, 260

Vertical structures of trust

Most industries, including that of textiles, don't have fully vertically integrated manufacturing models.[28] The financial risk is too high, and it has turned out much easier to create a vertical structure by employing companies, that employ companies, that subcontract to other companies.

Creating a vertical structure you don't control has its own implications. All these middlemen take a cut in the price build-up of a product, and each tier will add their cost and profit on top of the price they paid to the previous tier's product. Even more worrisome is that most final clients have no knowledge of the working conditions down the line, or of the pollution generated from their orders. And this has been a comfortable situation for the longest time. It was never considered the responsibility of the final brand. But this is rapidly changing. Many governments are looking into Extended Producer Responsibility (EPR) making each brand accountable for all that happens along the supply chain.

As we have seen in Chapter 6, it is in the interests of the garment industry today to keep people in poverty to maintain low costs and rising profits. This has created a very opaque structure in which systemic misconduct, and pollution with little regard the damages caused, have been ingrained.

Today the vertical value chain is top-down dominated. Brands control the prices. The expression, "It's a buyers' market", loved by re-

28. A vertically integrated production means that the company owns or controls the full manufacturing from raw materials to final product, including product marketing and sales. This is also known as backward integration. So if a company owns the field that grows the cotton, the ginning and spinning facility, the weaving and assembly unit, the design, has the marketing department and controls the final sales in their own (online) shop. This is not how the fashion industry operates today. Nobody controls the whole process from fibre growth to final sales.

lators is true in the manufacturing industry too. Companies push prices down, and this has a trickling-down effect, with each tier pushing down the prices of the tier below them. In this way the brand, client, can maximize profit and financial growth. It means that there is no equal partnership. Each transactional partnership is based on legal and financial relations, in which the buyer has the upper hand. This creates a value chain dominated by money, and pressure, not by trust or shared values.

The price we pay for any product reflects how we value it. When a price reflects the full cost, it would be effective in encouraging us to take care, appreciate and love our clothes more.

If we rethink the system bottom up, we create an exchange based on trust, and shared intentions. There is care for those participating in realising their ideas. It becomes a community of creators in which each has his role to play. This will give a sense of pride and fulfilment to each member of your community, creating a strong shared sense of responsibility. Many grassroot initiatives we see today operate like this. This results in less money being spent or paid to non-active shareholders, and while profit is lower or non-existent, there is more money and respect for the people involved in the process.

A relationship-based partnership looks very different from the inside looking outward, especially for those being exploited in the current system. They regain a seat at the table, and the financial incentive works both ways as a mutual exchange. These relations only function and exist in a trust-based setting. And relationships handle risk differently. In a community with mutual interests, risk is carried equally by all members, and all members collaborate in times of need.

With my brand we started out as buyers, purchasing time and materials, and using them however we saw fit. One thing that I always intuitively understood is that the technicians working on our clothes should always be listened to, and that negotiating the price we pay for labour should be avoided. I believe that if you find the right production partners, and they share your values and beliefs, as a buyer you should trust that the money, they ask for the manufacturing is based on sincere calculation and actual costs. This might sound foolish or naive to many in business.

We created these trust relations by being open and up front with our long-term visions and ideas, and by enquiring about the values and long-term goals of our potential partners. We explained that we wanted to operate from a position of trust. Any cost discussion would involve them as much as us, meaning that if the production price of an item was too high, we would sit together and figure out how to make it easier/less complicated to make. We only renegotiated when we knew the production price would lead to us not being able to sell the garment. When the sales price is too high, we all lose both of us as a brand as we will not sell anything, and them, the producers who will not be needed to make anything. It is therefore in our mutual interest to build a price that is fair and competitive.

This led to many situations where we as a brand have significantly reduced our share of the price, and sometimes even have revoked our part of the price, only breaking even on the style. We made this decision occasionally because we knew the supplier needed the business, or already made costs, and we were intent on getting them orders while aware that the sales price would not allow this. By taking our part of the price off, we could guarantee that our supplier's investment would be covered, and we would get to work with them another season. Of course, we met many producers who did not understand our opening question of transparency. Some thought they could start pushing prices after experiencing that we in fact did not fundamentally renegotiate the prices they requested.

It's a tough balance and you need to know how things are made, what their costs are, understand the market and recognize when you are taken for a ride. And you learn this by trial and error. Forming partnerships is an investment, just like any relationship. And it requires trust.

Trust is made up of two key elements – transparency and the ethics underneath what you do, how you do business. – Michael Beutler, director of sustainability operations at Kering

Once you lose trust in the fairness or openness of a supplier, continuing with them is hard. Providing transparency to enforce a feeling of fairness to both sides of the negotiating table is a strategy that has worked for us.

Developing a relation requires work, and time. But it is so worth it. We consider our suppliers as partners. They are our extended family. When political or economic circumstances occur in their region, we reach out and try to help from our side. During the Covid outbreak, we gave a part of our profit back to our Indian suppliers, understanding how hard it was for them when other customers pulled their orders without batting an eyelid. We talk about what their long-term aims are, what their needs and wants are in the aim of helping or facilitating them. We are generous in sharing the names of our manufacturers and suppliers with other brands, believing that if they have more business, it will be easier for them to fulfil their needs.

We have been working to establish the same lines of trust with our fabric suppliers. As you can imagine, moving up through the tiers is increasingly hard; the further away your sub-supplier is, the more complicated it is. So, we try to encourage our direct suppliers to create similar relations with the companies they source from, as we do with them. We are aiming to extend our family all the way to the farmer.

Operating in this way, we believe that we arrive with a real price, where all partners are payed fairly.

Transparency creates and maintains trust

One of the cornerstones to creating communities of trust and exchange is accountability. Each member needs to be open about their part. Lack of transparency on the impact you cause, the human and material resources you use act as a barrier and create distrust and suspicion.

The industry at large still operates in an unregulated global market where negative externalities can be produced freely,[29] becoming a 'footloose' industry that moves production to wherever it is cheapest, with strong vested interests to keep practices opaque.[30] Creating close-knit, trust-based relationships with radical transparency is a powerful force of transformation. Transparency provides a window into your everyday decision-making process and allows your partners to anticipate and predict your decisions. Those coherent decisions create the fabric of business that makes change possible[31], it creates trust.

Technology has a role to play in providing more efficient knowledge sharing possible as well as better tracking of materials and analysing impact of actions. Blockchain can digitally reveal the history of a garment's journey. This opens a possibility between the different chains in the making of valuable products, but it simultaneously enhances trust between users and providers. Those responsible for manufacturing are accountable for their actions, creating a trustworthy product for those looking to invest in the products or services produced.

Companies like Provenance have developed ID's that can hold location mapping, content, and timestamps for every step of the production process, making the full journey of a garment accessible via a smart label inserted in each piece, attainable for all via a QR-code. European policies don't allow for such state-of-the-art intervention to replace traditional composition tags yet. But the technology is available, ready for full-scale implementation at any point when the

---

29. A real price should reflect all negative external impact the product has, and any perverse subsidies should be removed. Ken Webster, The Circular Economy: A Wealth of Flows – 2nd Edition. (London: Ellen MacArthur Foundation Publishing, 2017)

30. Sophie Buchel et al. The transition to good fashion. DRIFT report. (Rotterdam, Erasmus University Rotterdam, 2018)

31. This thorough understanding of the necessity of transparency is what lead to Kering developing tools like their Environmental Profit & Loss program. (EP&L)

regulation changes. Till that time, any company aiming at transparency can provide this, alongside the mandatory composition tag.

Governments are important in facilitating change and supporting positive initiatives. They sometimes also move notoriously slowly. The industry does not need to wait and should not wait to see policy changes forcing them into new business strategies. Uniting as members of the fashion industry and behaving in the way you want to change towards is the most powerful tool each of us have. We lead by example. To enable community feelings, you need to share knowledge and discoveries. Enter the open-source mind set and let the world, and the people around you share in your innovations. Open-source concepts are already well on their way to becoming popular and more common and can help building trustworthy, reliable relations between people and communities thousands of miles apart.

Transparency is becoming the new normal. For companies, whether they're in luxury or any other industry, it's important that to communicate it in a positive way to better inform consumers and to help transform the industry. Everything you do matters; the embodiment of your values that support and care for the environment, support and empower people, that establish the outer and inner boundary of the doughnut as the horizon within which you operate.

Common Goals and Community Guidelines

Thinking in terms of communities, a strong base of like-minded people is your starting point. This might start small, and the values and ideas you want to implement might seem far out for many around you. Fortunately, humans can change and accept change at the speed of light. If you find the right core team, and start realising your ideas, the response will be overwhelming. Communicate about what you are doing. Your shared values and ideas are the base to create community guidelines, representing the standards which you work towards and aim for.

Starting small and local, is in this respect, a great advantage. Proximity creates strong connections. Shared beliefs are easily visible to all in the community. And the impact is bigger for everyone involved. More regional economies with a greater number of small-scale businesses that themselves have regional supply chains make more economic and environmental sense.

The fashion industry is highly fragmented. By creating cross-value chain collaborations, innovation and scale can be reached. When you partner with innovators, other brands, and manufacturers it allows you to identify and participate in scaling promising solutions. Invest in material research you see potential in.

It is the norm to invest in the development of interesting shapes, to invest in a design team – so why not invest in new technologies for transparency, material development and recycling too? And share your newly discovered knowledge.

The idea of this book emerged from this mindset. We realised that instead of sharing our contacts and discoveries with just one designer at a time whenever we attended a fair, we could collect all the information and knowledge that we had accumulated over the years and make it accessible for all.

Systems-thinking

An economy that is restorative and regenerative by design and aims to keep products, components, and materials at their highest utility and value always, needs to make a distinction between technical and biological cycles. This new economic model seeks to ultimately decouple global economic development from finite resource consumption and shift away from fossil fuel energy sources. These systemic changes will create new jobs, reduce environmental impact including carbon emissions and create a different type of growth. Positive growth, transgressing boarders and including care for all life on this planet.

The scale and speed of change required means that genuine systemic efforts are needed. In the fashion context this means addressing not only the environmental impact of a fashion product and the processes of making it, but also the psychology behind fashion use, our systems of economics, finance, and trade, how we design local and global infrastructures around clothing, and how we construct meaningful lives and livelihoods. Rethinking fashion outside the economic growth logic shifts power from multinational companies to organisations, communities, and citizens. It invites fashion creativity to flourish far beyond the confines of a garment, into visions of new relationships between people, other species, artifacts, and technologies.[32]

It will require unprecedented levels of collaboration and new solutions. To achieve it, the size and diversity of the network of people working on the subject need to increase, enabling ideas to travel to new places and creating wider understanding. Importantly, this broadening of the conversation will reveal new connection points in our global economy. Complex systems are greater than the sum of their parts, so these connections are where the magic happens.[33]

The beauty of system thinking is the notion all is interconnected via uncountable pathways, creating a spiderweb like structure where each actor is supporting and pushing all others forward. It links us all together making us experience our interdependency.

Fashion has a long history of creating experiences, providing people with a sense of belonging. This is exactly what fashion shows still

---

32. Kate Fletcher and Mathilda Tham, Earth Logic, Fashion Action Research Plan. (London: The JJ Charitbale Trust, 2019)

33. Tansy Robertson-Fall (sr. ed.) The role of art in driving systems change, Engaging more people in the circular economy discourse. (London, Ellen MacArthur foundation 2021)

attempt today: creating an experience that will become a memory that lives on long after the season. I still remember my first ever live fashion show; it was Raf Simons S/S 99 "Kinetic Youth"[34] and the magic, the tension in the air, the buzz of people, watching people watching clothes were magic and still fill me with excitement today. Other shows have left an equally big imprint in my mind and I will never forget them.

Fashion now has the great opportunity to create an even bigger experience. Audiences long to be part of positive stories that they can relate to, that visualize positive change and embody culture, rituals, and responsibilities. A network of local exchange and change that one can be visually part of as a distinctive manner of expression. Transnational networks that facilitate local exchanges of distinctive resources, materials, products, and knowledge.

Across many types of systems, diversity is a key driver of versatility and resilience. In living systems, for example, biodiversity is essential to surviving environmental changes.[35] Similarly, economies need a balance of various scales of businesses to thrive in the long term. The larger enterprises bring volume and efficiency, while the smaller ones offer alternative models when crises occur.[36]

---

34. https://www.youtube.com/watch?v=yQOo_ZIvaoo

35. In agriculture, contrasting with the industrial logic of efficiency and monoculture, recent experiments have demonstrated the benefits of leveraging biodiversity to improve crop resilience. David Baker, Post-organic: Leontino Balbo Junio's green farming future. In Wired, (Aug. 14, 2013)

36. Robert E. Ulanowics et al. Quantifying sustainability: resilience, efficiency, and the return of information theory. In Ecological Complexity Vol. 6, (2009) Pg 27-36

Redefine profit, growth, capital, and value

Economic growth is a man-made goal, and as such can be altered. In most economic textbooks growth and value are expressed in monetary terms: the price is what represents the value and is enabling quantifiable growth calculation.

Price should represent the value, but as we have demonstrated, in fashion it rarely does. Imagining an economy with a different approach to the dynamics of growth is a challenge. Fashion has a unique opportunity to invent the next step, to imagine the future from the ground up. Fashion is fundamentally creative, and parts of our fashion industry have embraced different business models already.

What if we radically turn away from the old growth-model? Some refer to the movement that is needed as degrowth. This is primarily because the Western, Educated, Industrial, Rich, Democratic citizens and nations have been overstepping their boundaries. We have been using far too much of our natural resources to be considered just, right, or fair, and with our unlimited polluting have put all of humanity at risk. Since the industrial revolution, human lives have changed dramatically. What was an exciting evolution with new opportunities has led to our excess production and prodigious waste today, creating a downward spiral of commodification with a culture of excess and blind consumption.

What if we think instead, in terms of value networks: interconnected, active, dynamic, and never-ending? What if growth and wealth simultaneously generate prosperity on environmental, social, natural and financial level?

And as a next step we don't address a value chain, which in its essence is linear enabling a take-make-use-dispose model, but instead talk about a value cycle. With this simple linguistic change value creation becomes possible at every step: the making, using, recycling, reusing, recreating. An endless cycle without the constant necessity of new materials being introduced at each consecutive manufacturing stage.

By using such values and ideals, we can articulate a greater economic purpose than monetary growth and create human growth, physical abundance, and social connections. This can, and should, be the new growth ideal.

Well-being can be promoted by connecting to the people around us, being active in our bodies, taking notice of the world, learning new skills, and giving to others.[37]

In contrast to consumption and bottom-line growth, words such as nurturing and caring imply very different relationships, including with fashion. Thinking bigger than the dress. Thinking holistic about the whole process. What do you want to achieve with this dress regarding the customer, the seamstress, the Earth, your bottom line?

Resource ownership

A very related but different question is this: who has ownership of resources?

Western prosperity is deeply rooted in our colonial past. We need to mend and repair these relations and approach potential partners with empathy. Show your vulnerability and be open.

If we accept that resources are limited, it makes each of us responsible for not wasting them or using more than our share. We can try to rectify this unbalance, by starting to pay local people a fair price for their resources, both in terms of materials and people.

Everybody deserves access to clean drinking water, everybody deserves access to sustainably cultivated crops, but it is the WEIRD who have gained the upper hand in terms of money, legal ownership and influence due to a colonial history that does not give them automatic entitlement to the limited communal resources around.

---

37. Centre for well-being, Jody Aked et al. Five ways to wellbeing. (London: New Economics Foundation, 2008)

Extended Producer Responsibility (EPR)

A few years ago, something extraordinary happened, and most of us haven't noticed. An in-store tax – known as an "electronic waste recycling fee" – was introduced to be paid by consumers on every electronics purchase. Its purpose was to cover the item's eventual disposal and made it mandatory for shops to take back all electronics from users, take care of their disposal, sending them back to the manufacturer. This happened without any protest or question asked and it is part of what we are collectively moving towards, namely an Extended Producer Responsibility (EPR).

EPR is a environmental policy and strategy thats adds all environmental costs associated with a particular product's life cycle to the market price of that product and make the producer of the end product either financially or physically responsible for the treatment or recycling after consumer use. Today this system is already implemented in sectors such as packaging, electronics, tires, cars, and batteries.

France is the only country in the EU using this today on clothing, linen, and shoes. Companies are obliged to either set up recycling and waste management systems for every item they put on the market or pay a contribution to an organisation that will manage their waste. Producers and importers are made legally responsible for the waste their product will become in the future. The French EPR organisation, ECO-TLC contributed to a threefold increase in the collecting and recycling rates of post-consumer textiles since its implementation in 2007. By implementing this responsibility, a direct incentive is given to eco-design. In France, any product containing a minimum of 15% of recycled fibres sourced from post-consumer textiles, receives a 50% discount on this tax. It directly promotes resale, rental models, take-back services and more. In this way, textile waste became valuable, and entrepreneurs saw a benefit in improving recycling quality and processes. As a side effect, companies also benefited from creating more high-quality clothing and longevity.

Nothing should stop companies from already becoming responsible for their waste streams, even before EPR becomes the norm in their country of operation. And under the EPR scheme it is advisable for a company to design their products for disassembly and recycling since they will be confronted with their goods again and again.[38]

With our brand, we set up a pre-loved section on our website in 2018 to enable customers to return their items and grant these items a second, third or fourth life. No criteria are imposed on the state of the garment upon return, but we do inspect, clean, if necessary, mend, and make each item look as good as new. We will assess it, and when it is no longer wearable, we will take care of its recycling. By setting up this system, we made our clothes accessible to a much bigger audience since the price of our pre-loved is 10-15% of its new value. The cost of the garment is already covered by the first buyer, and we want to enhance accessibility to all by keeping the pre-loved price solely the handling cost.

New models already in use

Economic business models which are purpose-driven and create benefit for all stakeholders, not just shareholders, are already up and

---

38. This is just a tool and by no means can solve the whole waste, overproduction and overconsumption problems. Reducing production volumes is not a core concern of the French EPR policy. To date, the average eco-contribution fee paid by producers per garment is just over €0.01. That does not cover the cost of managing post-consumer textiles. And it is not enough to be felt by either producer or consumer. Therefor the tax has no impact on the overproduction and overconsumption. There is no scaled recycling infrastructure that justifies reduced waste targets. There is still a long road ahead if we want to make the EPR help combat textile waste.

running. I have highlighted a few such initiatives, each operating in a specific section of the value cycle.

Each contribute to a product's life extension model extending the life cycle of clothes through repair, reprocessing, upgrading and resale. A piece of wisdom from ecological economy thought-leader Walter Stahel: "Reuse what you can, recycle what cannot be reused, repair what is broken, remanufacture what cannot be repaired."[39]

Share

Early 20th century marketeers did a great job convincing the public that the products we own, are actually products we use, and we actually use up. This is a vital shift in collective thinking because it enables a thought process in terms of disposals and using things up thereby creating a need for more, newer or a replacement of the outdated.

It seems only appropriated that for the last 10 years marketeers have been working for new companies, explaining to the public that we no longer need to own all our products, we can just have a community-owned product that is available when we need it, but that is shared in nature. Examples of this are everywhere: in big cities all over Europe buildings often have communal washing machines and dryers; there are books and toy libraries; car-sharing systems that are taking a bigger market share every quarter. And this thinking is taking ground in fashion as well. Subscription-based sharing platforms like ShareWardrobe and TheNuWardrobe, are experiencing unprecedented growth. Instead of your own, individual wardrobe, you have a communal wardrobe like a library, so you can choose a new garment to wear every day, at a fraction of the cost of purchasing it yet with the possibility of purchase and thus ownership.

---

39. Walter R. Stahel, The Circular Economy, in Nature, 531, 435-438 (March 23, 2016)

DESIGN FOR CIRCULARITY
Value cycle

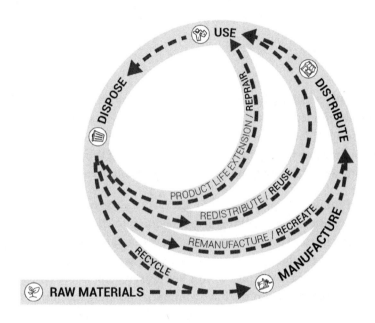

These initiatives are community-based exchange platforms where you sign up like library subscriptions, giving you access to the common space where you borrow what you need, and lend what you don't.

Swapping has been a recent community activity, taking place all around the globe, with each participant bringing a number of garments that can be swapped for other items brought by their peers.[40]

Rent

Similar to sharing are renting businesses with initiatives like Wardrobe being launched. This is a peer-to-peer fashion rental company which received backing from an Airbnb co- founder, and it operates on the same principles. We have seen these rental systems appear all over Europe for bikes and scooters and they are now also becoming common in the fashion world.

These business models move from pure ownership to performance-based payment models. They are instrumental in translating products designed for reuse into attractive value propositions. By prioritising access over ownership, they drive a shift away from consumers back to users and also allow an incremental increase in the number of wears of each particular item.

This trend started in occasion wear, protective clothes, and wedding suits and are now moving into baby and maternity clothing. Rentez-Vous or Rent the Runway still operate in high-end clothing, but initiatives like Nuuly, and Infinitely Loft are bringing the principle to a wider audience. As a client, you pay a monthly fee to rent a fixed number of garments at a time, making your wardrobe change frequently without buying new clothes.[41]

---

40. It is a creative challenge to find a way as a designer of fashion to operate in a sharing community. Maybe you share patterns or expertise?

41. The renting model comes with sustainable questions like how do users get the goods (shipment?) and how long do they keep them (if worn only once by each user, it has a big imprint on the dry cleaning performed after each user.)

Reuse

The EPR transforms most products to rented commodities, but companies have not fully realized this yet. The customer pays a price, receives the goods, and after use, returns it to the brand. That is, in essence, a renting loop. If this idea kicks in, producers and brands will see all the benefits of creating higher quality, long-lasting garments, and will start inventing ways of prolonging this life even more, before entering a recycling phase.

Companies are already offering customisation and styling services, all intended at keeping the garment in circulation longer by helping users see the full potential of their clothing and offering solutions to alter garments to individual needs. In this way, brands are building loyalty and improving the user experience. This system is based on Reuse on the Go, where a user can take an item to the store to have alterations done, receive styling advice or simply return it to give it a new life.

One company operating in this field is The Renewal Workshop. They are specialized in creating value for apparel brands from their in-shop returned items, implementing as a sales channel for high-quality, unwanted clothing. Founded in 2016, the company offers retailers a fully outsourced service, managing the reverse logistics, repair, cleaning, and resale of branded stock that customers return for any reason, whether the clothing is unused, lightly used, or in need of repair. Partnership fees for processing the clothing are comparable to what retailers would normally pay for waste management, but rather than disposing of the clothing, it is resold, either in-store by brands, or on The Renewal Workshop's website under a revenue-sharing agreement.

The longer garments circulate, with each time-added value, potentially provided by the brand, the brand earns money at every stage. When it turns it into waste, it can generate a new income, since it now is a valuable commodity as well.

Repair

Repair can be achieved in two different ways: at home, or professionally. Repair at home includes user-participation in the design or repair of clothing which fosters a more connected and active engagement with garments. It aligns with the idea that the quality of design increases if the person who ultimately uses the product is included in the design process.[42] This is known as the Ikea Effect: creating emotional durability. We love what we made ourselves even when the result is amateurish, and we value it like we value expert creations, expecting others to share our opinion.[43]

Professional services, such as shoe repair and clothing repair are not new concepts but are only now being explored as an efficient business model with growth opportunities. Established fashion houses offer in-house alterations and are moving into repairs no longer limited to patching up or improving the fit. Hurra Pangpang offered a full up-cycling experience during the 2022 Dutch Design week, clients would choose two garments to be merged together in a template way, creating a unique brand-new garment to be picked up later in the week.

42. Ellen MacArthur Foundation, Towards a Circular Economy, business rationales for an accelerated transition. (London, Ellen MacArthur Foundation, 2015)

43. Michael I. Norton, Daniel Mochon and Dan Ariely, The IKEA Effect: When Labor Leads to Love. In Journal of Consumer Psychology22, No. 3 (July 2012) pg 453-460

Recycle to remake

To promote recycling, brands like H&M already offer vouchers for any garment being brought back to their store.[44] This system is known as Return on the Go. Users are actively encouraged to return their garments by using deposit boxes and cross-brand collection points.

When companies really accept recyclable garments as valuable goods, return systems from home will also become common with organized pick-ups for recollection. Collection and reverse logistics companies that support end of life products being reintroduced into the system are being piloted even as I write this.

Addressing the barriers to clothing recycling is imperative. Whilst many organisations have begun to address technical issues, further work is required to close the loop in making clothing recyclable and putting measures in place to enable it to be recycled at the end of life. There is a reason that only 1% of garments are really recycled today.[45]

Several companies are working on clothing that adapts to changing user needs. Clothing that is designed to be multi-purpose, adaptable, and upgradable could increase the frequency with which customers use an item and lower the number of items they keep in their closet. There is an opportunity for designers to create modular garments that can be adapted by users over time. Garments that can be worn inside out, or that are made up of a fixed base together with remov-

---

44. There is a lot of controversy around those systems, since what H&M and other brands do with all the collected textile is very obscure.

45. There are many challenges and complications around recycling textile. I will get into this in the 2nd volume of Sew What, which will discuss several more "technical" sustainable fashion challenges and ideas.

able sections that are offered in multiple colours would allow one garment to match several outfit combinations.[46]

Fashion designers have been exploring this idea from a purely design concept, like Walter Van Beirendonck making a fully modular collection with pressure buttons to allow the user to remove sleeves, pockets reassembling the garment as they wish. There are already examples where this kind of multifunctional design is embedded in the brand's core or style. One such example is the Little Navy Dress, which consists of a 'blank canvas' onto which customers can zip decorative attachments. Adaptable materials that are easily upgraded represent a new area of innovation, whether they are garments that can be re-dyed or refashioned at home or are self-adaptive. For example, Petit Pli's children's clothes are pleated in such a way that they grow with the child and fit a wide range of sizes. At the more exploratory end of fashion, CuteCircuit garments include 'wearable technology', incorporating built-in images that are updatable through a mobile app.[47]

Custom-made

New technologies are emerging that adapt clothing to individual body shapes and styles, allowing custom-made clothing to be delivered at scale. Until the 1800s, 'made-to-measure' clothes were the norm and are still common in certain countries.

Globally, tailoring has become a luxury, being replaced by ready-to-wear mass market clothes in standardized sizes. New technologies are reintroducing made-to-measure on the mainstream market. 3D body-scanning technologies are already available to pro-

---

46. Ellen MacArthur Foundation, Towards a Circular Economy, business rationales for an accelerated transition. (London, Ellen MacArthur Foundation, 2015)

47. Ellen MacArthur Foundation, Towards a Circular Economy, business rationales for an accelerated transition. (London, Ellen MacArthur Foundation, 2015)

vide body-mapping analysis which, along with a fitting guide, could customize the perfect garment for the customer. Thus, on-demand manufacturing will no longer mean long delays to acquisition. For example, the Indian manufacturer quancious[48] offers customers a variety of materials and colours to choose from, and the second step is to assemble a garment from the base up: you choose the base garment type, the sleeves, the collar, the pockets etc from an extensive list of design options. A few days after completing the online order, the garment is ready for delivery.

Locally distributed production through the sale of designs online that can be 3D-printed locally and easily assembled by the customer is another innovation that has the potential to create products only where and when they are needed. Such a model is currently operated by the Post-Couture Collective in Belgium. On-demand manufacturing could also reduce brands' need to discount or discard overproduced items.

Slow fashion

Unlike fast fashion, slow fashion is an attempt to convince consumers to buy fewer clothes of better quality and to keep them for longer. The philosophy includes reliance on trusted supply chains, small-scale production, traditional crafting techniques, using local materials and trans-seasonal garments. It calls for a change in the economic model, towards selling fewer clothes. Azzedine Alaïa was one of the first major fashion designers that stopped producing according to the main fashion calendar, instead releasing collections when he decided they were finished, however in recent years this idea has been replaced for standard seasonal collections again.

The platform Betabrand allows anyone to submit a design idea, crowdfund it, and produce it if the idea proves popular thus removing unneeded, overproduced goods, and only moving into production

---

48. Www.quancious.com

when the community gives a clear indication they want the design to be made.

———

What all these initiatives have in common is that their focus is on meeting the needs of present users without compromising the ability of future generations to meet their own needs. They are all searching for ways to create emotionally durable items that are highly valued and cared for by its owner.

For far to long the fashion industry has chosen fast over slow, more over less, enabling exploitation and depletion.

Sustainable business practices are rooted in an understanding that empowering workers, protecting public health, and preserving our ecosystem are part of one and the same effort.[49] Sustainability accepts that resources are finite, and should be used conservatively and wisely with a view to long-term priorities and consequences of the ways in which they are used.[50]

---

49. Jedediah Britton-Purdy, Environmentalism Was Once a Social-Justice Movement. It can be again. In The Atlantic, (Dec. 7, 2016)

50. UCLA Charter What is Sustainability? Sustainability is the balance between the environment, equity, and economy. (Los Angeles: University of California, 2019)

If creativity drives social and economic change, it is the designer's job to use storytelling to clarify those values and ideas about connected communities of makers.[51]

---

51. For further reading on a sustainable economic future, I have relied on the ideas of functional service economy (performance economy) of Walter Stahel; the Cradle to Cradle design philosophy of William McDonough and Michael Braungart; Biomimicry as articulated by Janine Benyus; the Industrial Ecology of Reid Lifset and Thomas Graedel; Natural Capitalism by Amory and Hunter Lovins and Paul Hawken; the blue economy systems approach described by Gunter Pauli, the fabulous work of the Ellen Mc Arthur foundation and the all-encompassing Doughnut economy ideas expressed by Kate Raworth.

A DURABLE ECONOMY THAT IS SUSTAINABLE

• Community thinking, become part of a resilient families of makers

• No longer taking natural resources for granted. They have infinite value if treated well.

• Vertical lines of trust and transparency, communication and exchange are key.

• Visualising value at each step of the cycle, imagine how your intervention is adding value.

• Consider waste as a design flaw, your design should not be destined to become waste.

• Replacing growth pure sang by care and mutual growth.

Eight

Redesigning the world one idea at a time

REFLECTING ON MY DESIGN methods seems so intuitive because design is at the core of my work. The design stage is where a new reality is shaped, every season, every month, and every day.

During many years of concept coaching and teaching aspiring fashion designers how to develop their ideas, I have evolved a few ground ideas of how creative flows work. And yet often, I'm still caught off guard by how easily unexpected connections just seem to make sense in a design, or even in my head.

The imagination is a beautiful and scary place which some people have an easier time accessing than others. Every creative person who relies on it for their work, experiences the irrational fear of one day being confronted with no new ideas.

Normally, I start a collection six to seven months prior to displaying it in a showroom for shops to place their orders. The first step is a random gathering. Looking around, investigating, visiting places I like, that alter the way I see things is how I gather physical mementos, keepsakes, emblematic relics: napkins, postcards, little toys, leaflets, found objects. It's a very arbitrary collection of things that possess a certain beauty that struck me.

I also take digital photos, but mostly only use them for colours and details, but rarely for more. In the office, there is a big box, full of little *objects trouvés* – things that bring joy, inspiration, and that are part of my memory library.

Around three weeks into the process, all the collected items are filtered, and a selection emerges from which the story of the collection is told. In the atelier we have images of direct visual inspiration, colours, textures, techniques, and sustainable challenges and ideas. Things we want to experiment with, want to improve, bring more into the collection. Sketches are made, styles are drafted, and a full set of sketches is ready for the team to be translated, into patterns, tests, technical files, prints, block printing, etc.

It will take about three months for all members of the extended team to complete their part. Our factories sample the patterns in a first prototype (in the final materials), ready for photoshoots, fairs, showrooms, and buyers. Another month is spent setting up photoshoots, look-book shoots, creating the marketing material and teasers for buyers, and then sales season starts. By that time, I have long detached myself from the collection, and I will have already been at least two months into the next collection process.

Our team is a well-oiled machine; if one chain doesn't run smoothly, all the rest get blocked. And if creativity is not leading the way, the next in line have no job.

Design blackout

It happened to me once in Season Five. Judging from the press, models, and customer response it was a very successful collection. But its conception was the hardest labour of love I ever created.

That season, when the time came to design the next collection, my private life was a mess, scattered in emotional pieces. As the result of a new relationship, I felt as though I was redefining myself through someone else's eyes, influenced by their gaze. Not a safe place from which to design and create.

The very week when I needed to start designing the next collection, we broke up and unfortunately, the result was that I questioned everything in a way that I never had before. Every little thing I drew, every image I liked, each fabric I related to. It was as if my private redefinition had invaded my professional life and left me incapable of deciding anything. All was at risk, all was under suspicion, all was questioned, and I had no confirmations or negations.

After drifting like this for several weeks the pressure started building. There are specific times-slots attributed to my designing the collection and we should have already been about three weeks into testing and developing. Yet, every day I continued to doubt, and had no designs ready. My team had no work and we lost valuable time that would be virtually impossible to catch up with at a later stage of the process.

The stress of paying a team doing nothing, whilst being in full existential crisis over everything was horrific. It was the most terrible moment in my professional life, yet it was also the moment I learned the most.

When I had nowhere to turn to anymore, and was in the depths of despair, I finally reached out to two fashion designer colleagues, who had many more years of experience and had no relation to children's fashion. They both responded to my cry for help with generosity, genuine advice, and time. It was an eye-opener to realize that in this very competitive industry, help is at hand if you ask for it.

I travelled to Paris, with a little fitting doll on my back, and a suitcase full of toiles, prototypes, tests, and half-started ideas.

Once there, I ended up spending over two hours talking to Lutz Hulle, who comforted me and explained why Collections Four through Six are so hard. It's the first time you have an actual feedback loop from customers; the reality of your endeavour is starting to kick in; it asks a lot of questions you might not have been confronted with earlier. This can be so overwhelming that it paralyses. We discussed the goals of the brand, and he helped me examine it and its core values instead of being blinded by the collection at hand.

Josephus Thimister and I spent two magical days in his house, going through everything, creating aesthetic family groups, looking at the red line, identifying little stories within the big story. We sketched missing scenes, and we threw out ideas that were great but didn't fit this story. It ended with all the samples and drawings on the floor, inspiration images included, and us crawling in between, reorganizing, regrouping, until it all made sense, until one general image emerged that was by no means logical, but which felt coherent and right.

It taught me to rely on the process and the vital role of including others to find solutions if the problem overwhelms you. You are only as strong as the totality of the team you work in.

Simultaneously I learned the importance of listening to all feedback loops, while keeping an eye on the horizon. The bigger picture painted by our values, purpose and vision must always be a leading principle.

Let me first clarify that when referring to design and how things are made, I am defining design in broad terms: from the micro level of designing a material or redesigning how materials are used and made – via the actual product, or ways to re-use it – to the experience around the product to the business model in the background; all be designed.

Going forward the term designer can be understood as fashion designer, but is not limited to it.

In the same sense, I define good design as design that only delivers positive impact.

A new job description for (fashion) designers

Until today, the job of a fashion designer has been pretty well-defined but rather limited. It seems insufficient to tackle today's challenges. Any designer, better yet, any person with a creative mind and a motivation to tackle problems could enter this conversation of sustainable fashion, and how it should look moving forward. Change might well come from the outlier, the one with the disruptive idea and limited fashion background. It might even be easier for them, as they are not restricted in their ideas of what a fashion designer's "traditional" job is. Those free to play with fashion codes, confident to reuse existing fashion resources in new configurations are liberated to investigate new pathways out of our current ways of creating fashion.

Historically, the function of fashion designer grew from tailors, seamstresses and technicians. Innovation and creativity were celebrated, but with a technical skill set as the underlying foundation.

Technicians have a problem-solving mindset from the start. They configure and reconfigure information time and again to find the best assembly methods for all the elements. A tailor making a made-to-measure jacket, will collate all his years of experience, mix it with the specific design wishes of this customer, add the customer's measurements, and figure out the best way to assemble this specific jacket. Factually, he is blending his sense of aesthetic, knowledge, and experience to create the best possible jacket for this specific order.

As time went by, and the industry grew larger, and opaquer, jobs became more specific. Today we have fashion technicians using their knowledge and experience to develop other people's ideas. And we have designers, creating lush dresses and shapes, with little concern about how and by whom they will be made. We can find ourselves surrounded by teams of specialists on just about anything from marketing to material innovation. As long as designers are regarded as the top of the food chain, with no demand to become a humble part of the system, these specialists cannot support a drive to good design.

It seems as though all we expect of fashion designers is that they freely design what they want. As such they are barely confronted with the distress of our industry. Just recognizing one fabric from another, is deemed to be sufficient technical knowledge. And the only problems they are required to consider is what body they are dressing, and what aesthetic they want to pursue. The technical problems will be solved by the pattern makers and seamstresses; the sustainable problems will be solved by an independent department, or another tier in the supply chain.

This mentality is deeply ingrained in our teaching systems. Fashion design students are still closely located to the art section, having freedom to create, with minimal material and technical knowledge. Fashion designers are often only required to practice image thinking and free association, which leads to art rather than product. And fashion designers by definition are designers fashion, hence designers of objects. It requires more than just images and aesthetics to create objects and it needs more than simply logical-rational deductive thinking to be innovative. What is required of fashion designers seems limiting, patronizing, and insufficient for the challenges of our industry today and tomorrow. A designer has so much more to contribute to the world than this.

It is disappointing that those people who enjoy finding solutions, who are trained to be creative, feel that they are not challenged to use their skills to the best of their abilities. Imagine the gratification if they could not just decide on a skirt length, and invent a new sleeve, but simultaneously tackle an actual industry problem, and instigate impact along all supply tiers, manufacturers' lives, as well as the world.

One of the biggest designers of the 20th century described design as "a plan for arranging elements to accomplish a particular purpose".[1] That does not limit the job of a designer to choosing the material and the volume around the body but makes it potentially much more expansive. It implies that we should define our purpose, the "why" that motivates our work. And the bigger the purpose, the larger the potential impact.

---

1. Short movie, Design Q&A, Questions by Mme. L. Amic. Answers by Charles Eames1972, on the occasion of the exhibition "Qu'est ce que le design" at the Musée des Arts Décoratifs, Palais de Louvre. (1972, Charles and Ray Eames. 1992, 1993 Lucia Eames Demetrios dba Eames Office.)

"Design is not a craft for industrial purpose, but it might be a solution to some industrial problems. Design is not a discipline that concerns itself with only on part of the environment."[2] – Charles Eames

To design our future, a great designer needs to have a profound understanding not only of human desire but also of each aspect of the fashion industry, and a collaborative mind that is eager to exchange and learn from everyone in the supply cycle. Do not just focus on a collection; keep an eye on the bigger picture.

Concepts must be value-based

In essence a designer is a problem-solver for a difficulty that has multiple possible good solutions. The key is choosing the innovative creative one that suits both your purpose and concept, solves the problem, and produces as few new problems as possible.

In a way this design job description is paradoxical since it requires a designer to innovate, while retaining a certain level of conservatism. A dress should still be a dress, not pants. A new table needs to function as table and be recognizable as such, while appearing new and innovative.[3]

Each new fashion collection originates today from a concept, a set of visual guidelines for the pieces, colours, fabrics, shapes, and presentation. The concept behind the collection either applies to the model, the whole collection, or the brand and should not be limited to the purely visual aesthetic.

---

2. Short movie, Design Q&A, Questions by Mme. L. Amic. Answers by Charles Eames 1972.

3. Augustine noticed already that latin has two verbs for "I think" namely Cogito "I blend together, picture, ponder" and intelligo "I choose between". Gerda Smets et al. Beeldspel, Ruimtelijk inzicht en beelddenken. pg 52

It is rather regretful we have never given fashion designers the opportunity and tools to use their minds for what it does best; find alternatives, search for solutions, invent new things. To really excel at that, we need to confront them with the existing problems and demand new propositions; from the drawing board.

The concept behind a collection, or a company, can be the guiding principle for all the action. Not just leading the aesthetic but more fundamentally, also the ethic decisions. That implies that concept and company values align, and they mutually reinforce each other. Central to all practices, from the decision of the pants over the skirt, the length, and also the way it is made, by whom, and where can be derived from this value / concept combination. They question and show how you want the company to be run and what kind of collections you want to make.

Fashion thrives on an aura of magic, a wizardry behind or even in front of a curtain, a magical invention of new shapes and forms that make people dream. In this myth, we ignore the second part of the job at hand: to find solutions to problems. To invent novelties in your practice.

At some stage, the job might become less appealing for a lot of current fashion designers, but maybe that is just an evolution needed to fundamentally change and disrupt our industry. It is a designer's job to know and identify problems and create solutions. The two collections a year, are almost a by-product, or collateral benefits. There needs to be evolution, more than just the raising and lowering of the hemline, and the broadening and narrowing of the shoulders or the plunging of the neckline. We need to start demanding more, much more of them. Challenge and inspire them!

It cannot only be about aesthetic, and how it looks; it needs to be an all-round better product. As a designer, we impact how our product takes shape, how it will be worn and experienced by the wearer, and the consequences of their use. A designer should be proud of the design in all its facets.

———

Companies bombard designers with questions about concept, season, material, and shape for the season. They don't ask what problems need to be solved. It is time to stop being afraid of confronting fashion designers with their biggest challenges. Figure out what needs to be improved, what needs to be reinvented.

By seeing and feeling the impact and problems your generated ideas, you can start to imagine change. It is my belief that this harsh reality is hidden to designers. The confrontation with the impact of your actions is vital to understanding your impact. The reach of your ideas, so you feel how much a better idea would affect the world you operate in. In this respect the collection that is designed is only a side-effect. The actual result of your actions is much bigger than that. Seeing this reality is essential for beginning to think out of the box for good impact designs. The garments and productions each season, are merely testing and optimizing better ways of making things and evidence of the fact that it can be done better.

At my atelier, each season kicks off with a reflection on the feedback we received. We reflect on our actions. We identify where our purpose could be better supported by our actions. And the concept of the collection is a blend of aesthetic inspiration, and well-defined problems we want to solve, shine a light on, or a cause we want to support. We are a fully organic brand. The logical implication is that our crops that generate our fibres are not treated with chemicals, thus enhancing biodiversity, and creating cleaner waterways.

One season we decided to highlight this by dedicating the visuals of the collection to insects, those little creatures that we don't kill when growing our textiles. Their world inspired our shapes, textures, and artwork. Simultaneously we decided to make it at the core or our marketing efforts of that season, organizing marches at each fair, to ask for a pesticide-free future. It made us question how we could go beyond and really improve biodiversity, and it started our quest for multi-crop farmed fibres -- something we never investigated before.

The concept of that specific collection influenced our processes, our sourcing, and we decided to contribute directly to children's education about organic methods, and the bee conservation efforts made by bee sanctuaries. It improved our long-term functioning by making us aware of something we never focused on before, improving biodiversity beyond the organic into regenerative. Our purpose and values each season are an integral part of the aesthetic, and each season we learn and discover new paths to improve our functioning.

Having clear a purpose, and concepts that integrate the purpose and values you hold dearly, drive good solutions to even better ones.

Inspire optimism

The inkling that inspires each season, that motivates designers to make new things is big enough to aspire fundamental innovation.

I look all around me for inspiration and it is not fashion that inspires my next collection. The solutions and innovations presented by designers are so small, and often very disconnected to what could be. A pretty dress, with no further fundamental reflection is just a missed opportunity, creating more of the same problems we already have. It fails to ignite any aspiration in my world or work.

Those thinking out of the box are the ones that use design as a disruptive game changer to its full potential. They light my fire, push my thinking forward, and make me search and mentally investigate new roads to improve practices and challenge conventional methods.

Fashion professionals benefit from an underlying principle in their work, to make it relevant, and impactful. A clearly defined value framework, a manifesto, an expression of vision, that will lead good design on many different levels. Good design is not limited to the next dress; it has the potential of finding better answers to the challenges the world faces today. In that respect, the canvas of design can be used to address many problems of our industry, creating ideas that offer the promise of more effective solutions. That dress might be more cost effective, that might be impactful all the way around the value cycle, that might ignite fundamental change on a small or big scale. Then that dress carries the promise of a whole new world, it carries the promise of a positive impact. It inspires optimism and motivates other people to reach the same kind of promise in their work.

I am inherently optimistic. To take on big challenges, especially like the ones our industry is facing, we need to believe we have an impact. It is essential that we believe there are answers out there, even if we haven't found them yet. Even if they have not been invented yet. By identifying a problem, by highlighting a situation, multiple people can focus their mind on finding good solutions.[4]

We have created our world, shaped it, with all our current problems included. If we can create all this, then it seems more than logic that we can also create alternatives for obstacles we have incorporated in our world. Constraints exist in many ways and forms, but they can push designers towards unexpected solutions. A design thinker translates ideas and insights into products and services that will improve lives[5]. On another level, design thinking can improve the lives of those involved in the making culture.

Blank canvas

Starting from a white canvas every season for every new drawing, forces the designer to adopt a beginner's mindset and search for new insight about the object you are about to create, and the user that might wear it.[6] You have an almost absolute impact on how your

---

4. IDEO, The Field Guide to Human-Centered Design. (San Francisco: IDEO, 2015)

5. Tom Kelley, The Art of Innovation, Lessons in creativity from IDEO, America's leading design firm. (New York: Currency Books, 2001)

6. Eli Woolery, Design Thinking Handbook, DesignBetter.co by InVision. pg. 10

products take shape, how clients will experience them, how they will feel while wearing them, the consequences and impact of the garment's use, and you have a tremendous impact on all the people that are involved in the realization of your products, for better or worse. You have the power to improve biodiversity or further destroy it. The choices you make on that blank canvas carry all this potential. It is not to be taken light-heartedly. It requires knowledge, compassion, and a different mindset to see new possibilities and alternatives not yet explored.

You have a chance to use your privileged opportunities with empathy and compassion, and design products that you're proud to bring into the world, knowing they will create positive impact, far beyond the primary consumer.[7]

Unlike in many other industries, we fashion designers don't often start with a defined problem. But maybe we should; maybe our problem should be a particular unethical practice, or unsustainable staple, and the search should be on how to improve this, while implementing it into a whole new garment that functions as a vehicle of ideas, as proof that change is possible, and desired. As an opportunity to illustrate a point of view.

I believe, after years of experience, that creativity is like a muscle. If you practice it, your output grows, and the quality of your work gets better. If you challenge your creative thinking, it starts flowing. The more diverse or ephemeral your outlook and thinking are, the more likely that you can find multiple solutions for the problem you are facing[8]. Once you enter a creative borderless state of mind, thoughts and solutions start appearing from all places.

7. Eli Woolery, Design Thinking Handbook, DesignBetter.co by InVision. pg. 110

8. Gerda Smets et al. Beeldspel, Ruimtelijk inzicht en beelddenken. pg.10

A particular state of mind

Thinking often is categorized as primary and secondary,[9] otherwise known as divergent and convergent thinking.

An example of the first is a dream, associative and inductive, focussed more on similarities and undifferentiated. It is typically non-linear, free-flowing and exploring multiple solutions simultaneously.

The second type is logical and deductive in nature, focussed on the differences between the objects of your thought. Rational and hierarchically organized. Ideas and information are organized and structured, approached in a deductive manner.

Thinking in images is a huge help in generating new ideas. But judging the ideas on feasibility and impact also requires logical-rational, technical, and systematic thinking.

The process of ideation, or designing ideas and solutions, is characterized by an alternation between both types of thinking, the divergent and convergent thinking. Both need to be activated to creatively approach challenges. Primary thinking allows for the more absurd, out of the box kind of ideas to surface, while secondary thinking can see the thought through to its extremes, analysing its possible implications and effects. At the one end, experience and observation are needed; at the other end, they should not be controlling your thinking to the point where you get paralyzed and can no longer freely associate and create.

To find solutions for any problem or challenge it is essential that you are aware of the problem. That seems self-evident. Fashion designers need to know the full extent of their impact, to design better pathways. If you don't know an issue exists, none of your energy is ever focussed on improving it or finding alternatives or solutions.

---

9. This devision started with Freud, and was later elaborated on by Carl Jung, and Werner.

Design thinking

In essence, design thinking permits us to tackle complex challenges, and imagine solutions. Design thinking includes processes like context analysis, problem finding, ideation, framing, solution generating, sketching, prototyping, testing, and evaluation.[10] Design thinking is especially useful when addressing complex problems. The design thinker explores the problem at hand and might re-interpret or restructure it, to reframe the problem so as to discover a potential solution. Often the approach will lead to a co-evolution of the problem and the solution. Design thinking is today a globally heralded approach in every industry, from tackling politics over biochemistry to banking, and healthcare services. It is used to think about every part of our lives. To speculate, evaluate and observe any part of our society, and imagine improvements.

The system of design thinking is not actively used in fashion design. While it should be used to radically rethink supply chains, to reimagine the materials we use, fashion designers are not bothered with it at all. If this kind of design thinking could become mainstream in fashion design, if problems and solutions could co-evolve, it might lead to a very different industry. Most problems today only exist because they are designed. If fashion designers understood the complex and unsolved problem of a blended cotton-polyester material, would they still use it?

The absence of design thinking in fashion design might be a big reason why sustainable solutions in fashion take so long to be found or implemented. Company CEOs often talk about expressing purpose and intention, incubator hubs inside the company brainstorming about possible pathways. But the sustainability dilemmas are placed in separate departments, each with their field of expertise. Why are the designers, the problem solvers not invited, or even required to enter this discussion? This isolated bubble of designers is outdated.

---

10. Nigel Cross, Design Thinking. Understanding how designers think and work. (Oxford: Berg, 2011)

Sequestered from the rest of the company they lack input, inspiration and cannot be part of the solutions. How can a concept be value- and purpose-driven, if the situations at hand are hidden from the designer or creative director defining each collection?

It supports the old persistent way of thinking, that making fashion sustainable is a matter of the technician, or the material expert, a problem the designer is not supposed to be bothered with. It fails to recognize that the problems of our industry will need imaginative design thinking to identify them and visualization to see solutions.

To design a good product, the end of life needs to be created in unison with the products genesis. And at conception of the product, no materials should be used without a clear end game. This poses the first design question: will this product follow cradle-to-cradle thinking in its material choices? Will it be designed for disassembly? All other questions and choices flow from there.

Imagine yourself in the middle of a desert. In every direction you look there is sand. And straight in front of you is an arrow pointing you in the right direction. But this arrow will not determine the type, size, and content of the solution. Your brain will, in combination with the vibration of the air. Choosing to make a product biological or technical says nothing about the shape the product will take, but your associative brain will; it will find inspiration in unexpected places and in its unique combinations shape a new object of desire.

It's one of the most fascinating things. We all work in the same world. We watch television, YouTube, listen to music, see art show, movies, the news. And yet it all influences us in endlessly different ways. Our creative minds will find pathways of combining different information to create. These combinations are unique to each of us, but strongly embedded in local and global commonly shared cultures and history.

Character

I have had the privilege to observe and work side by side with many talented creative problem solvers in various industries: engineers, chefs, politicians, thinkers, and designers. They all have a few things in common. They understand their metier. They are liberated from prejudice in thinking and don't censure themselves halfway through the process. Every thought is pursued to its extreme limits, served from all angles, tweaked, and altered until satisfaction is attained. They are not afraid to start from zero, and they welcome feedback.

Anyone can approach the world as a designer.[11] With a little creative confidence anyone can think as a dynamic problem solver.[12] Everyone designs who devises courses of action aimed at changing the existing situations into preferred ones.[13] A few core competences are however vital to operate as a designer of change.

Perseverance

Surprisingly often, I will see a problem without any solution on the horizon. Dreaming up new ideas, envisioning challenges in a new light, adapting designs to collide with a solution for the challenge. It helps me to focus on multiple problems at any given time, finding

---

11. Enzo Manzini, Design, When Everybody Designs. An Introduction to Design for Social Innovation. (Cambridge, The MIT Press, 2015)

12. IDEO, The Field Guide to Human-Centered Design. (San Francisco: IDEO, 2015) The team of IDEO identifies seven mindsets that amount to wild creativity, a ceaseless push to innovate and make fundamental innovation tangible: Empathy, Optimism, Iteration, Creative Confidence, Making, Embracing Ambiguity, and Learning from Failure. I agree with this list yet added a few qualities.

13. Herbert Simon, The Sciences of the Artificial (Cambridge: The MIT Press, 1969)

solutions to some of them while selectively focusing elsewhere. I find it allows my convergent and divergent thinking to collaborate, flaring out into all possible directions while remaining focused on specifics at the same time. Some problems will require our suppliers to get involved. Some are much bigger and will require multidisciplinary teams or even industry-wide collaboration to find solutions. But stay vigilant, a proposition might pop up at any moment, from anywhere.

The tabula rasa at the beginning allows for innovation, lasting impact, and a freedom to pursue all potential pathways to answers. And to hear all voices at the table.

In my team we have a firm focus on where we want to go, what we want to realize, what values we are pursuing. We waste little time pondering over the obstacles on the road there.

By rethinking the problem, the view is altered making a holistic and free approach possible. Reframing gives the opportunity to define the problem as a project with determined goals. This does not mean we know the solutions; the goal is the result of the solution. The goal clearly outlines the direction of our search.

Empathy

Our value chain is so scattered over the world, and the designs we make impact so many lives, that to solve problems on all levels, you need to be able to see the world through their eyes. Those people have knowledge that will prove essential for solving certain issues. By putting ourselves in the shoes of all the different collaborating partners, we can start to see the world, and all opportunities to improve it, through a new and powerful lens.[14] It also allows you to get rid of old presumptions and preconceived ideas based on old fashioned

---

14. IDEO, The Field Guide to Human-Centered Design

ways of doing fashion. Showing an openness to all people involved generates a collaborative state of mind.[15]

Humility

Nobody will solve our shared future alone. A designer is only a member of his team, and listening is often more important than talking. Exchange will allow values to grow into strong guiding principles for the team, however big or small that might be. Collaboration is key.

Understanding strength in numbers

Parallel to a humble understanding of the role of the designer, co-learning and group knowledge are important forces to be deployed. When everyone feels responsible for the final positive purpose, knowledge will flow in all directions, across generations, communities, and companies. Within a company, interdisciplinary teams will have the biggest chances of success.

Open access to knowledge and expertise beyond your own can be exchanged to serve the mutual goals. Within an extended family of teams working together, ideas can bounce around, supported by all the skills, capabilities, and knowledge of each participant, at every tier. Empower collaboration with your peers, with NGOs, with academia, and with governments. We all need to collaborate with other business sectors and start-ups to drive innovation. By looking at design as a Darwinian human product, we can grow and learn from our shared past to design out the problems and improve with every step.

In a broader sense, the more people and companies that ask for a specific solution, the bigger the economic value of such product becomes, encouraging more companies to start looking for appropriate solutions. We have always shared information on all our suppliers

15. Kate Fletcher, Craft of Use, Post-Growth Fashion. (New York, Routledge, 2016) undefinedJonathan Chapman, Emotionally durable design. (London, Earthscan, 2005)

and manufacturers. Ensuring a steady supply of customers finding their way to our suppliers has been our best guarantee that our suppliers remain committed to their sustainable program, and this indirectly secures our supply-cycle for the next season.

Creative confidence

It demands a lot of confidence in your creative abilities and your intuition to continue going, in the face of failure, confronted with uncertainty and problems than sometimes appear unsurmountable. Chasing a solution, without any insurance that your idea will eventually work, exploring ideas that up to date gained no new insight. Design largely depends on constraints. Designers can recognize as many of the constraints as possible – price, of size, of strength, of balance, of surface, of time, of impact, of resources, etc – while enthusiastically working within them.[16] Each problem has its own peculiar list of constraints that challenges a designer to overcome them. As designer, leaving my comfort zone to get excited about the impact I might have in the world is what motivates me every day.

Some of the problems we have identified in our team have taken us years to solve. Finding the right partner to recycle our cutting waste took so long, that for more than eight years, our cutting waste was pilling up in my basement and office corners. We were determined to find a working solution and finally we successfully found partners in Tilburg and Paris.[17] But rest assured, during those eight years, I often found myself doubting if we would get there or if I would end up living on top of an ever-growing pile of fabric scraps. A holistic mindset is what kept me going; it is not about the one garment, or the one collection, there is the ideal of a better industry that pushes our thinking forward.

---

16. Short movie, Design Q&A, Questions by Mme. L. Amic. Answers by Charles Eames1972.

17. undefined

As a fashion designer, it would be possible to design your clients home interior with their dress like Henry Van De Velde did. But holistic design can also be understood as designing the process that makes our fibres, how we grow them, the way we make our clothing, together with the actual garment.

Visualizing the problem in front of you makes it possible to observe the situation that surrounds the issue. In your mind you can analyse, illustrate, and express solutions. After this first step, try your idea for real as soon as you can.

Manufacturing trials

In our industry, making samples to try our drawings, and improve the fit has always been the norm. We make prototypes to optimize the manufacturing quality and to show our ideas to potential customers. Today more and more companies are working with digital simulations to replace the need for actual resources to be used.

Prototyping can be done in any form as long as the ideas are visualized sufficiently to analyse them from all angles. Also, ideas need to be made, tested, and potentially adapted to improve their functioning. By adopting an iterative and varied approach at every new trial, new vital feedback becomes available, potentially improving the hypothesis, slowly distilling ideas into concrete solutions that are working while embedded in the community. Accepting that the first trial will not be perfect, you can focus on getting all parts right over time.[18]

Designing anything, including solutions for intangible problems like worker rights, is hardly ever a linear process. It is not a sequence of improvements. It happens in a more evolutionary manner, with chaos, trial, and error. It is like taking two or more independent facts, ideas, insights, or elements and combining them in a constellation.

18. Eli Woolery, Design Thinking Handbook, DesignBetter.co by In-Vision

After this initial act the structure will be adapted and optimized multiple times. A collaboration between the initial idea, the feedback of each prototype and the problems surrounding the prototype will lead to a viable positive product.

During our whole collection-making process we talk and exchange with the manufacturers, suppliers, children trying on the prototypes and their parents, to optimize and change to initial idea to the final product that responds to all needs and requests raised in the best possible way. The making of the product is the sum of all the impactful solutions we have uncovered along the way. And sometimes this means taking unexpected turns along the development.

Failure and error

In the quest for great products, and long-lasting impact along our manufacturing cycle, failure is an inevitable part of the process that we can learn from. Since we don't know the result at the beginning, and we use each prototype as a learning curve, we don't regard them as failed garments, but rather as visual research elements that allow us to sharpen and refine our ideas and the ways we are formulating answers. Exploring and testing permits the acquisition of knowledge. The insights of what does not work reveal so much about what might work. The better we observe the first samples and feedback, the faster we can start tackling the presented problems and explore unexpected alternative pathways. By prototyping, you avoid guessing and assumptions. Testing is meant to reveal problems and mistakes, so test to fail, learn and adapt. But, simultaneously, have an next-life solution what will happen with your test after you are done.

Ecological literacy and respect for locality

Design and imagination are an attempt to add products, services, and ideas to our world. It is a living process and a force that starts with acknowledging the reality of today. It can shift our attention away from the self-preoccupied belief that 'the earth has no planetary boundaries I have to adhere to', focusing outward on our interdependency on others.[19]

By being able to identify the problems, teams can be built to focus on finding new approaches, of collaborations with suppliers, technicians, contractors, supply cycle partners working together for a better outcome. If the request/need for alternatives is not formulated, and sent out there, no other specialized textile engineer will be inspired to work on a solution.

Vocalizing your request for alternatives is a powerful motivator for competing suppliers to help you realize your aim, so they can win the bid for your order.[20] State your intention. It also means you can be held accountable. And there is nothing wrong with ambition to realize a sustainable future.

The environmental crisis is a crisis humanity has created and designed.[21] In order to solve it, environmental and community priorities must dictate the purpose and values of companies, and thus establish the industrial ambition and scale of every collection developed, within natural and human limits.

Since not every ecosystem or community is the same, the activities within them require adaptation to the specific place. Since India is responsible for 70% of all organic cotton grown worldwide, it is logical to make cotton garments in India. Our atelier in Germany is highly qualified to make our small series, they enjoy the variety and change of work. This type of localism, relating to the faces and places involved creates dynamic creative forces for long-term prosperity within the specific site.

19. Kate Fletcher and Mathilda Tham, Earth Logic, Fashion Action Research Plan. pg.36

20. William McDonough and Michael Braungart, The Upcycle: Beyond Sustainability – Designing for Abundance. pg 9

21. Sim Van der Ryn and Stuart, Ecological Design. (Washington DC: Island Press, 2007)

By thinking local, it favours the use of nearby resources, place-specific knowledge, community self-reliance. It gives expression to practices shaped by traditions, necessity, climate, imagination and a distributed form of authority, leadership, and political power. The secure rooting in the community enables generous sharing of knowledge, skills and resources as opposed to any protectionism and company trade secrets. Because fashion operates in so many locations, what is made and how, will look different in each place. The available resources will be different in each location and by involving and communicating with the community responsibilities will be carried by all.[22]

In understanding the local situation and changing procedures, products, site-specific designs, a new design dynamic will become prevalent. We talk to each factory extensively, before, during and after each season, to figure out what they specialize in, to understand what kind of challenges make them happy, what kind of materials are nearby and local for them, and we design around these resources. Each factory we work with, will receive a specific design series, fit for their skills, expertise, and location. We try to maximize the available social assets and materials to serve the local community and our brand vision in harmony. It is a process of co-creation and aligning ideas.

The power of storytelling

For a company, a story is a potent way to communicate values and objectives across a widely dispersed and multicultural organization or system.[23]

---

22. Kate Fletcher and Mathilda Tham, Earth Logic, Fashion Action Research Plan. pg 50

23. Tom Kelley, The Ten Faces of Innovation, Strategies for heightening creativity. pg. 245

Expert storyteller, Stephen Denning, advocates using the right kind of narrative, to be matched with the right situation.[24] Authenticity here is key. Storytelling is a great way of sharing insights about your values, purposes, achievements, and ideals. Make the story authentic: if you advocate change, make it part of your life, in your company, in how you address problems. Let it become part of who you are so intrinsically, that without it, you no longer would be the same.

Stories can have focused purposes in your business like sparking action, transmitting values, fostering collaboration, or leading people into the future. Before you begin a story, it's important to know what specific outcome you are hoping to attain.

Build a strong narrative to change the mindset of those around you. Your story has the power to create teams of like-minded people, beyond company borders. So, tell it in an enchanting, whimsical, motivating way. Show the people around you the impact they might make.

I'll never forget meeting a farmer who told me why they went organic, and how me using their materials not only paid their livelihood, but as a result of my purchasing their organic cotton, they and the extended family could now work in a safe, healthy environment, with no fear of the illnesses which had plagued them when they were using chemicals on their fields. I felt proud, honoured to be part of their established wellbeing. Their story holds such power for me, that I feel my impact, with each order of organic fabric. Even if I'm ordering in another country from another supplier. The meta message expressed the impact of organic purchasing on the farmers.

Remember how you tell your story, what medium, what focus. – for yourself, your team, the world. You need to make everyone feel why this is vitally important. And create a clear call to action. Be detailed, persuasive, specific. Embrace and mention any scepticism or contro-

---

24. Steve Denning, The Leader's Guide to Storytelling. Mastering the art and discipline of business narrative. (San Francisco: Jossey-Bass, 2011)

versy, air common doubts and worries, and then knock them down, one by one. Storytelling can act as a Trojan horse, getting past our initially defensive reactions of doubt or scepticism, and enabling us to have an open discussion about a relevant idea.[25]

An authentic story tells an underlying truth and is a fundamentally human way of conveying information.[26] Storytelling is part of the fabric of humanity. Stories create passion, insight, and true connection. Thinking about any project or problem in terms of a story permits exploring extravagant, controversial situations and answers.

Fashion designers, like other designers, are trained to tell stories. Through collages, mood boards and drawings we tell stories to our teams, helping our team bond. Through shows and photoshoots, we tell stories to our clients. By incorporating game-changing ideas wrapped into compelling stories we can create a paradigm shift within our team, within our extended family, and in the world, widening our sphere of influence.[27]

Storytelling provides a vocabulary for change. And it helps make order out of chaos. It can express your ideas for a roadmap out of today. The garments we create breath our stories, they are the collateral benefit. Meant for people to enjoy, and a non-invasive way to advocate radical change.

Every fashion lover longs for "a beautiful thing that does not harm the world but instead has been designed *for* it."[28]

---

25. Tom Kelley, The Ten Faces of Innovation, Strategies for heightening creativity. pg. 252

26. Tom Kelley, The Ten Faces of Innovation, Strategies for heightening creativity. pg. 247

27. Ellen MacArthur Foundation & IDEO, The circular design guide.

28. William McDonough and Michael Braungart, The Upcycle: Beyond Sustainability – Designing for Abundance pg 73

Criteria

Design makes an important contribution to the preservation or destruction of the environment., depending on how it is deployed. It can conserve resources and minimize physical and visual pollution throughout the lifecycle of the product while incorporating a non-invasive end of life, if you conceive it that way.[29]

Conscious designers today are focused on a variety of good practices such as minimizing waste, enhancing cyclability, reducing chemical impact, reducing energy and water use, exploring better / cleaner technologies, promoting ethical production, reducing the need to consume, promoting dematerialization, developing services and systems. Some designers create participatory design, and some use their design as activism. And this is just touching the surface of good practices being explored today.

Define what triggers you most. Tell your story, draft your roadmap, and start drawing change.

Develop your list of what constitutes Good Design within your work field. Below is my list, though it is by no means complete. We add, alter, and specify each season, depending on the projects we are focused on. We find that our criteria are like a double helix, intertwining our knowledge about the processes, people, and nature, with our values and purpose, leading to our own highly personal distinctive approach to our work.

---

29. Dieter Ram expressed 10 rules of Good Design in 2018, Although I believe it is a wonderful list of rules, they also imply certain aesthetics, which make them less fitting for fashion today. Make your own list of what constitutes good design for you. #

Good design is innovative by nature, co-creating a beautiful object and an abundant future.

Good design makes a product useful; a product is bought to be used. It must satisfy certain criteria, not only functional but also psychological and aesthetic.

Good design is positive and unintrusive in its impact throughout its full life cycle, being an integral part of nature's system.

Good design is executed well, enabling longevity, aesthetic pleasure, and functionality; it has the possibility to stand the test of time.

Good design is thoughtful and thought through, honest to the extended family about its origin, heritage, and value.

Good design starts with intergenerational justice and involves all who directly and indirectly act in relation to the object, activity, or service.

The relationship between fashion, design, and sustainability is complex, and there are many methods and approaches you can choose. The good news therefore is, that there are many excellent ways of moving forward.

It is your duty to remain determined to improve and evolve and stop falling into the old destructive ways of doing fashion.

Design tools

There are several design tools on the market today, employing creativity to implement change. I have found the following to be very helpful to start a sustainable design journey

Circular design guide

The guide is a collaboration between the Ellen MacArthur Foundation and IDEO and is intended to help people understand the context for sustainable fashion and encourage them to create new solutions, both in terms of sustainable consumption and through sustainable co-creation. The website contains many worksheets, intended to get you started.[30]

CFDA Guide to Sustainable Strategies

A comprehensive guide to different strategies and the role of each member of your extended system.[31]

Sustainable Design Cards

This deck of cards is open source and highlights the different paths available to designers to change and optimize the sustainability practices in their company. It can be used as a toolbox to navigate the complexity of the issues and it offers tangible tools for better design.[32]

---

30. https://www.circulardesignguide.com

31. CFDA, Domenica Leibowitz et al., Guide to Sustainable Strategies. (Council of Fashion Designers of America, 2019)

32. Ulla Ræbild and Karen Marie Hasling, Sustainable Design Cards: A Learning Tool for Supporting Sustainable Design Strategies. in: Niinimäki, K. (Ed.), Sustainable Fashion in a Circular Economy. (Helsinki: Aalto University, 2018) https://sustainablefashioncards.com

Afterword

Thank you so much for reading this book till the final sentence! I hope it was both inspirational and motivational. Get started, ask questions, and implement small changes that have big impacts. And when you are ready, pick up Sew What ?!? Volume 2. After finishing book one, you know everything about the core topics, how to design for Planet, People, and Profit. Now you are ready for the particulars. In the second book, I dive into the details.

Volume 2. discusses the following topics:

- Form in a design vocabulary indicates shape and volume. And defines what parts are not formed; the cutting waste, the out-of-fashion, and the trash. Waste is becoming valuable, a new source of income, as it used to be before our society became a throwaway society. Designing patterns in new ways can reduce or eliminate waste. Designing for disassembly makes recycling easier. Using C2C thinking facilitates recycling. Which materials are possible to recycle, and how? Cotton, polyester, wool, leather, and cashmere. Blended fibers make it virtually impossible.

- The texture is a fiber affair. Will the 20th century go down in history as the polyester age? There are so many fibers and fabrics out there. Listing them all is an endless endeavor since about 150 new materials hit the market each year. So how do you assess the sustainable impact? Understand what the raw material that makes up the material is and what its origin is? – investigate if your material is processed chemically (transforms the material) or physically (alters the material) – what additives are used – how is the fiber turned into textile – how is the fabric turned into the color and texture you like. The use and after-life phase influence its circularity. At every stage, ask how and where and look at the collateral impact.

- Body, oppression by cloth. The body is the center of the fashion designer's universe; it is the canvas of the design. So why has the canvas been reduced to one shape, size, and form? The abstraction of the human body helps industrialisation but destroys our uniqueness, that fashion likes to rave about. And to a much more devastating extent, the animal body has been suppressed to indulge in every fashion fling. The scale of animal suffering to fulfill fashion dreams is staggering and has a tremendous ecological footprint. Greenhouse gas emissions, air-, water-, & soil pollution, deforestation, and declined biodiversity. Fashion is not using a byproduct; it is the reason most fashion-supplying animals are bred, kept, and killed.

- Cost of color. Chemistry is at the core of making most textiles and almost all colors. But where does nature turn into chemistry? And is chemistry the enemy? No. The invisible engine pushes innovation and will be detrimental to converting our industry to a sustainable one. So what is the difference between toxic and safe chemicals? Open-source knowledge exists, and positive reinforcement will go a long way. Green chemistry will identify chemicals of concern and push to design them out of your products. So only positive chemicals remain.

- Proportion; how important is a correct measuring tape. The measuring tape is the best friend of any garment maker. The tool you use to measure matters. Especially when moving towards sustainability, you need to measure your impact. There are tools to measure your impact. And there are standards to compare your estimated data with. To judge any tool or standard, understand how they work. Case studies:

Life cycle assessment, Living wage calculator, high index. Blockchain, in its build-up, helps us secure the collected data, build upon it and present it as trustworthy.

- Energy. What are sources of energy? Greenhouse gases are destructive to the environment and are a logical side effect of our use of fossil fuels. Calculating our carbon footprint and aiming at carbon zero is crucial in fighting the climate crisis. Find your biggest energy consumers, shift to renewable energy, reduce energy use, and optimize energy usage. First, internally, and then help your suppliers. Look at modes of transport, building use, heating and isolation, the different textile processes, and their water and energy use.

- What's next? My hopes and dreams: I plan to lead by example and keep learning. Advocate for change. It is not complicated. It requires determination, knowledge, and action. Use my brand Infantium Victoria as a testing ground for new ideas and move our collections to entirely biodegradable, compostable garments. Optimize the recycling of our cutting waste and keep our garments in circulation as long as possible. And by being fully transparent, use the collection to demonstrate that fair wages, GOTS certification, and fashion can seamlessly go hand in hand. The overall aim is a world where sustainability is no longer a privilege but the norm, accessible for all, creating a healthier, happier, and prettier place in the process.

When you are ready, I look forward to meeting you in volume 2. or in person.

Dinie

Acknowledgments

Even as a child, I knew my profession would be in fashion. Many people have shaped my thinking and guided me with their insights. It took me some time and wandering around to find my niche, but I finally made it home.

Early on, my grandmother, Oma Smits Taconis took my fashion idea seriously and chaperoned me to my first fashion show in Paris.

Hieron Pessers recognized my eagerness to learn and enter this realm and taught me more than I could ever ask for. Our days together were always filled with conversations about shape, body, volume, and craftsmanship.

To this day, I hear Josephus Thimister in my head, coaching and encouraging me. I am so grateful for the wisdom and insight he graciously shared. But even more special was all the critical questions he had, questioning me as a means to help me find my voice.

Writing this book has been a fantastic journey. So many people have gracefully shared their expertise and ideas. I am terrified I will fail to mention a crucial voice in my process; when I do, I'm so sorry.

From the beginning, Albin Kaelin from EPEA Switzerland has shared his knowledge and expertise. And giving me the priceless feeling that he is always just a phone call away.

Joseph Maire has patiently explained all I never knew about energy and the sustainable possibilities ahead of us.

Ralf Gubler reminded me that chemistry is the scientific study of the properties and behavior of matter and, as such, is neither good nor bad. It just is.

Winfried Heininger from Kodoji Press, thank you for the advice, patience, and direction in a domain I knew nothing about. I still hope one day, we can make a beautiful collector's item of this book together. Who knows, a girl can dream.

Dessy Tsolova from Fashion Insider, you gave me the little push I so much needed to take the final step in finishing this book. Thank you for sharing your knowledge so generously.

Sooni Gander, my editor, what fantastic work you did! My manuscript was much like a newborn puppy, enthusiastic and energetic, with urgent need of some order and discipline. Thank you for bringing your expertise and transforming my baby puppy into this version I love.

Atticus Technical support team, thank you for saving my book. When I thought the book would never finish, you found the bug in my format and pulled my project back afloat.

I feel blessed to be surrounded by people who have listened to my endless thoughts, ideas, and doubts. Giving feedback, encouragement, and suggestions when I needed them most; thank you, Olivier Maire, Mara Rodriguez, Mikhail Rojkov, François Schaeffer, Dr. Alexandra Schuessler, and Gerda Van den Bergh.

Very grateful to Claudia, Blandine, Erwan, Rami, Doug, Mathilde, Lucie, and my dad; each of you has been invaluable in pushing my work forward.

I have been honored to be part of a few of the world's leading fashion institutes, full of knowledgeable colleagues at ESEDS Kolkata, HEAD Geneva, and IFM Paris. They are training the next generation, which holds so much optimism and creativity that it makes me very hopeful.

It was a refreshing experience to have my first manuscript reading at HEAD long before the manuscript received this final form. Thank you for the trust you endowed me with.

Special shout out to Aloke Singh for your pioneering work at ESEDS. Proud to be a small part of your revolutionary institute.

Amanda Johnston from The Sustainable Angle, thank you for creating the amazing sustainable textiles platform! And entertaining all my creative impulses, hosting our game, exchanging ideas, and stimulating my book project.

Fernanda Hernandes, each time we talk, it's like an explosion of positive energy, pushing my sustainable targets further every time. So grateful for the encounters we have shared so far. I hope for many more in the future!

It was a blessing to meet Brian Iselin from Slave Free Trade. Exchanging with you confirmed my conviction that people are the core of any sustainable practice and must be cherished. Our conversations have pushed my thinking and questioning further than ever.

Jonathan Ohayon from F.A.K.E., you have built an amazing platform dedicated to kind, peaceful, and animal-free fashion. The impact of being supported by like-minded people should be considered. Thank you for the feedback along the way.

Niki de Schryver and I go way back. I have witnessed firsthand how sustainable fashion in Belgium, and by extension Europe, has progressed due to all the amazing projects, ideas, and companies you have created. So happy to still be on this path parallel to yours and able to exchange concepts when needed. Thank you!

My first public appearance with the book has been supported from the start by Suzanne Vock, founder of GWAND festival. Thank you for creating the fantastic festival to promote sustainable fashion, and thank you for giving me a platform to address your audience. The public reading when the book was just a manuscript convinced me of just how many people are interested and looking for reliable information. It has been a pleasure to talk on panels during your festivals, challenging my preconceived concepts on sustainable topics. Thank you, Tania Schellenberg; I know you are in charge of the speaker list, and I was very fortunate to be included in the last few editions!

I'm incredibly grateful for the countless times the Infantium Victoria team stepped up, granting me time to work on my manuscript. Taking care of day-to-day operations, guiding our lovely interns, and ensuring our philosophy comes to life with every collection we develop. Imani, Maaike, Aline, Aviva, and Grimaud, two thumbs up. PS. Love my artwork. Great job, Grimaud!

Our office has been blessed with hard-working and curious interns that constantly push my sustainable thinking to the next level.

Externally, we at Infantium Victoria work with excellent suppliers and factories that operate at the forefront of sustainability. Always ready to exchange ideas on improving operations, techniques, and the final product. It's such a blessing to be working with you! Each and every one of you has always been willing to educate me on your craft and specialty. I have learned so much!

Thank you! Varun Mehra and the amazing Nagesh Knits Family, Mihir Batra, Nitin Batra, Ashwani Palaha and the incredible team at Fabstract, Girish G. Krishnan and the team at Impex Clothing, Padmini Govind, an extraordinary leader of the very talented block printers at Tharangini Studio, Shankar D. Gowri and Elen Tsopp inventors and producers of Weganool, Benjamin Itter, co-founder and our amazing partner at Lebenskleidung and Marita Bartelet, founding pioneer at Ecological Textiles.

Giuseppe Grillo, thank you for devouring every word I wrote long before it was a coherent text, taking the time to consider every draft and formulate your feedback and encouragement. Who could ask for a more beautiful token of love?

This book would never have been written without Julia Gaydina, my Infantium Victoria business partner in crime; if you didn't have this dream for an organic vegan children's collection ten years ago, who knows where I would have trailed off too. You are a driving force, always embracing my new crazy ideas and finding ways to realize my dreams, even if I don't fully understand them yet. Sustainable world domination is one step closer today!

I finally made it to the last people on my list; thank you, Mom, for the trust, freedom, and support to make my dreams come true without hurting Mauritz in the process.

And Mauritz, I could not wish for a better son; your courage and perseverance inspire me every day. It is not easy having a mother who travels around and whose work is her favorite hobby, but thank you for believing in my ideas and accepting that I needed so much time alone to write this book. I hope to contribute to a beautiful world for you to wander into. Love, mum.

About Author

Meet Dinie van den Heuvel, published author, experienced educator, sustainability coach, and fashion designer. As the Head Designer of Infantium Victoria, a pioneer in designer sustainable fashion for kids, Dinie has set an industry example for a sustainable approach to kids' fashion.

The idea of "SEW What?! How to Design Sustainable Fashion?" was born out of Dinie's encounter with numerous brand owners and fashion designers, who were curious about her remarkable sustainable expertise in running a designer fashion brand. Through her discussions and panel talks, Dinie realised that the industry was crying for change, yet there needed to be more information available for decision-makers and practitioners on how to do it. As a result, Dinie is set on a path to share her more than 15 years of sustainability practice with a wider audience.

As a professor in various top-ranking schools in Europe, Dinie has an extensive network of students who have landed positions in major fashion houses worldwide. However, she saw the frustration of her former and current students who were looking for and could not find the proper tools to change their design approach, specifically embracing sustainability. She sees her book as a first step into shifting the approach to fashion design. SEW WHAT is a book that designers, aspiring and established, to change their framework, liberate them from stigmas around sustainability in fashion and create a better world.

"SEW What?! How to design sustainable fashion?" stands out from other books on the market as it provides a comprehensive guide for designers who want to make a difference. Unlike other books on sustainability topics, it offers a fundamental framework for designing sustainably. This is the book for change-makers. Join the tribe!

Bibliography

Books

- Edwin A. Abbott, *Flatland, A Romance of Many Dimensions.* (Mineola: Dover Thrift Editions, 1992)

- Kip Andersen and Keegan Kuhn, *Cowspiracy, The Sustainability Secret.* (San Rafael: Earth Aware Editions, 2016)

- Aristotle, *Constitution of the Athenians,* Athenaion *Politeia* 12 *.4, quoting Solon*

- Artistotle *Physics,* 209b 20-33

- Steve Beckert, *Empire of Cotton: A Global History.* (New York: Vintage, 2015)

- Edna Bonacich and Richard Appelbaum. *Behind the Label: Inequality in the Los Angeles Apparel Industry.* (Berkeley: University of California Press, 2000)

- Andrew Brooks, *Clothing Poverty, The hidden world of fast fashion and second-hand clothes.* (London: Zed Books, 2019)

- Jonathan Chapman, *Emotionally durable design.* (London: Earthscan, 2005)

- Nigel Cross, *Design Thinking. Understanding how designers think and work.* (Oxford: Berg, 2011)

- Herman E. Daly and Joshua Farley. *Ecological economics: principles and applications.* (Washington DC: Island Press, 2011)

- Charles Darwin, *The Formation of Vegetable Mould, through the Action of Worms, with Observation on their habits.* (London: John Murray, 1881)

- Lieven De Cauter, *Ending the Antropocene, Essays on Activism in the Age of Collapse.* (Rotterdam: nai010 publishers, 2021)

- Steve Denning, *The Leader's Guide to Storytelling. Mastering the art and discipline of business narrative.* (San Francisco: Jossey-Bass, 2011)

- Joanne Entwistle, *The aesthetic economy of fashion. Markets and values in clothing and modelling.* (New York: Berg, 2009)

- Kate Fletcher, *Craft of Use, Post-Growth Fashion.* (New York: Routledge, 2016)

- Kate Fletcher and Mathilda Tham, *Earth Logic, Fashion Action Research Plan.* (London: The JJ Charitbale Trust, 2019)

- Peter Frankopan, *The New Silk Roads: The Present and Future of the World* (London: Bloomsbury, 2018)

- Masanobu Fukuoka, *The One-Straw Revolution, An Introduction to Natural Farming.* (Emmaus: Rodale Press, 1978)

- Masanobu Fukuoka, *The Natural Ways of Farming, The Theory and Practice of Green Philosophy.* (Madras: Bookventure,1985)

- Arthur Haberman, *The Making of the Modern Age.* (Toronto: Gage Publishing, 1984)

- Giorgos Kallis, Giacomo D'Alisa and Federico Demaria (ed.), *Degrowth, A Vocabulary for a New Era.* (New York: Routledge, 2015)

- Tom Kelley, *The Art of Innovation, Lessons in creativity from*

IDEO, America's leading design firm. (New York: Currency Books, 2001)

- Tom Kelley, *The Ten Faces of Innovation, Strategies for heightening creativity.* (London: Profile Books LTD, 2006)

- Jeffrey Kopstein (ed.), . (Cambridge: Cambridge University Press, 2014)

- Michael Lavergne, *Fixing Fashion: Rethinking the Way We Make, Market and Buy Our Clothes* (Gabriola Island: New Society Publishers, 2015)

- Enzo Manzini, *Design, When Everybody Designs. An Introduction to Design for Social Innovation.* (Cambridge: The MIT Press, 2015)

- William McDonough and Michael Braungart, *The Upcycle: Beyond Sustainability – Designing for Abundance* (New York: North Point Press, 2013)

- William McDonough and Michael Braungart, *Cradle to Cradle: Remaking the Way We Make Things* (London: Vintage Books, 2009)

- Kristen Ohlson, *The Soil Will Save Us: How Scientists, Farmers and Foodies are Healing the Soil to Save the Planet.* (New York: Rodale press, 2014)

- Raj Patel and Jason W Moore, *History of the Wold in Seven Cheap Things: A Guide to Capitalism, Nature and the Future of the Planet* (Oakland: University of California Press, 2017)

- Plato, *Timaeus,* 50e

- Maria Puig de la Bellacasa, *Matters of Care: Speculative Ethics in More Than Human Worlds.* (Minneapolis: University of Minnesota Press, 2017)

- Kate Raworth, *Doughnut Economics: Seven Ways to Think like a 21st-Century Economist* (London: Random House Business, 2018)

- Hans Rösling, *Factfulness: Ten Reasons We're Wrong About the World and Why Things Are Better Than You Think.* (New York: Flatiron, 2018)

- Dr. Vandana Shiva, *Earth Democracy: Justice, Sustainability, and Peace.* (Berkeley: North Atlantic Books, 2015)

- Herbert Simon, *The Sciences of the Artificial* (Cambridge: The MIT Press, 1969)

- Hernando de Soto, *The Mystery of Capital: Why capitalism Triumphs in the West and Fails Everywhere Else.* (New York: Basic Books, 2000)

- Gerda Smets et al. *Beeldspel, Ruimtelijk inzicht en beelddenken.* (Delft: Delfste Universitaire Press, 1994)

- Kassia St Clair, *The Golden Thread, How fabric changed history.* (London: John Murray, 2018)

- Kassia St Clair, *The Secret Lives of Colours.* (London: John Murray, 2018)

- Douglas K. Stevenson, *American Life and Institutions,* (Stuttgart: n.d., 1987)

- Karen Tranberg Hansen, *Salaula: The World of Secondhand Clothing and Zambia.* (Chicago: University of Chicago Press, 2000)

- Greta Thunberg et al., *The Climate Book* (Dublin: Allen Lane, 2022)

- Ken Webster, *The Circular Economy: A Wealth of Flows – 2nd Edition.* (London: Ellen MacArthur Foundation Publishing, 2017)

- Sim Van der Ryn and Stuart, *Ecological Design.* (Washington DC: Island Press, 2007)

Articles

- Jane Abray, *Feminisme in the French Revolution.* In The American Historical Review. Vol. 80, No.1. Art.3 (Oxford: Oxford University Press, 1975) https://www.jstor.org/stable/185905 1

- Kevin Anderson and Alice Bows, *Beyond 'dangerous' climate change: emission scenarios for a new world.* In Philosophical Transactions of The Royal Society A Vol. 369 (2011) Pg 20-44 https://www.flemingpolicycentre.org.uk/Anders onBows2011.pdf

- George Arnett, *How much more would you pay for a sustainable T-shirt?* In Vogue Business, (Oct. 1, 2020) https://www.voguebusiness.com/sustainability/ho w-much-more-would-you-pay-for-a-sustainable-t-shirt

- Katy Askew, *Cost pressure "threatening survival" of European milk production:* EMB (Dairy reporter, May 12, 2022) https://www.dairyreporter.com/Article/2022/05/12/cost-pr essure-threatening-survival-of-european-milk-production -emb

- David Baker, *Post-organic: Leontino Balbo Junio's green farming future.* In Wired, (Aug. 14, 2013) https://www.wired.co. uk/article/post-organic

- Sébastien Barot, Alexis Ugolini, Fadia Bekkal Brikci, *Nutrient cycling efficiency explains the long-term effect of ecosystem engineers on primary production.* In Functional Ecology Vol 21 (2007) http://millsonia.free.fr/publications/barot2007F uncEcol.pdf pg. 1-10

- A. Berger and M. Loutre, *An Exceptionally Long Intergalcial*

Ahead? In Science, Vol. 297, issue 5585. (August 23, 2002) h ttps://www.science.org/doi/abs/10.1126/science.1076120 pg 1287 – 1288

- Steve Boggan, *'We Blew It': Nike Admits to Mistakes Over Child Labor.* (The Independent, Oct. 20, 2001) https://www.commondreams.org/views/2001/10/20 /we-blew-it-nike-admits-mistakes-over-child-labor

- Anna Brismar, Seven forms of sustainable fashion. https:/ /greenstrategy.se/seven-forms-of-sustainable-fashion(Accessed Feb 08, 2023).

- Jedediah Britton-Purdy, *Environmentalism Was Once a Social-Justice Movement. It can be again.* In The Atlantic, https://www.theatlantic.com/science/archive/2016/12/how -the-environmental-movement-can-recover-its-soul/5098 31/ (Dec. 7, 2016)

- Sophie Buchel et al. *The transition to good fashion.* DRIFT report. (Rotterdam, Erasmus University Rotterdam, 2018) https://drift.eur.nl/wp-content/uploads/2018/11/FIN AL_report.pdf

- Michael Braungart, William McDonough and Andrew Bollnger. *Cradle-to-cradle design: creating healthy emissions – a strategy for eco-effective product and system design.* In Journal of Cleaner Production xx (2006) https://cdn.vanderbilt.edu/vu-my/wp-content/uploads/site s/3191/2021/04/13135815/EcoEffectiveness-main.pdf pg. 1-12

- Anna Canadell et al., *Sustainability Handbook for Resilient Fashion Business 2023*, Inspirational Sustainability guides Bcome, https://bcome.biz/resources/sustainability-handb ook-for-resilient-fashion-business-2023/ 2022

- Susan Cosier, *The world needs topsoil to grow 95% of its food – but it's rapidly disappearing.* (The Guardian, May 30, 2019) https://www.theguardian.com/us-news/2019/m

ay/30/topsoil-farming-agriculture-food-toxic-america

- Renee Cho, *Why Soil Matters.* (Columbia Climate School, State of the Planet, April 12, 2012) https://news.climate.co lumbia.edu/2012/04/12/why-soil-matters/

- John H. Cushman Jr. *International Business; Nike Pledges to End Child Labour And Apply U.S. Rules Abroad.* (The New York Times,   May   13,   1998) https://www.nytimes.com/1998/05/13/business/internatio nal-business-nike-pledges-to-end-child-labor-and-apply -us-rules-abroad.html

- Olympe De Gouges, *La Declaration des Droits de la Femme et de la Citoyenne.* (Sept. 15, 1791) https://web.archive.org/web/20211103043613/https:/ /www.olympedegouges.eu/rights_of_women.php

- Sarah Ditty et al., Fanzine issue 01, *Money Fashion Power* (n.d.: Fashion Revolution, CIC 2017)

- Sarah Ditty et al., Fanzine Issue 02, *Loved Clothes Last* (n.d.: Fashion Revolution, CIC 2017)

- Emily Farra, *Regenerative Agriculture Can Cahnge The Fashion Industry – And the World. But What Is It?* In Vogue (May 12, 2020) https://www.vogue.com/article/regenerative-agricu lture-sustainable-fashion-christy-dawn-fibershed

- Emily Farra, *"Transparency Will Get This Industry Back on Track" – A New Swedish Label is Raising the Sustainability Bar.* In Vogue (May 21, 2020) https://www.vogue.com/article/a mendi-swedish-denim-label-sustainability-transparency

- Emily Farra, *What Is The Right Price For Fashion?* In Vogue, (June 29, 2020) https://www.vogue.com/article/what-is-t he-right-price-for-fashion

- Diane Francis, *Mending the capitalist model. Tau Investment*

Management in partnership with Alex Soros and other well-heeled Americans are raising US€1-billion to clean up de world's worst supply chains. (Financial Post, June 27, 2014) https://financialpost.com/opinion/in-bangladesh-tau-inve stment-management-hopes-to-spur-a-race-to-the-top

- Vanessa   Friedman,   *The   Biggest   Fake News   in   Fashion.* In   The   New   York Times https://www.nytimes.com/2018/12/18/fashion/fas hion-second-biggest-polluter-fake-news.html (Dec. 18, 2018)

- Yessenia Funes, *Yes, Colonialism Caused Climate Change, IPCC Reports,* in The Frontline, (04.04.2022) https://atmos.earth /ipcc-report-colonialism-climate-change/

- John Geisei, *10 Ways to Conserve Topsoil.* (July 21, 2017) https://homeguides.sfgate.com/10-ways-to-conserv e-topsoil-13406977.html

- Isabelle Gerretsen and Ivana Kottasova, *The world is paying a high price for cheap clothes.* (CNN, May 6, 2020) https://edition.cnn.com/2020/05/03/business/chea p-clothing-fast-fashion-climate-change-intl/index.html

- Bob Giddings, Bill Hopwood and Geaff O'Brian, *Environmnent, economy and society: Fitting them together into sustainable development.* In Sustainable Development, Vol. 10 No. 4. pg 178-196 (n.d. John Wiley & Sons, Nov. 2002) https://www.researchgate.net/publication/227650507_Env ironment_economy_and_society_Fitting_them_together_in to_sustainable_development

- Gary B. Gillis, *Snail Trails.* In Journal of Experimental Biolo-gy, Vol 210, Issue 17 (Sept. 2017) 10.1242

- Richard Gray, *Why soil is disappearing from farms.* BBC, part of the Follow the Food series. (July 19, 2019) https://www.bbc.com/future/bespoke/follow-the-fo

od/why-soil-is-disappearing-from-farms/

• Deborah Hardoon, Sophia Ayele and Ricardo Fuentes-Nieva, *An economy for the 1%: how privileged and power in the economy drive extreme inequality and how this can be stopped.* (Oxfam International, 2016) https://policy-practice.oxfam.org/resources/an-economy-f or-the-1-how-privilege-and-power-in-the-economy-drive -extreme-inequ-592643/

• Arthur Harrop, *Thousands of low-paid retail workers are getting stuck, not getting on.* (London: Trade Union Congress, May 3, 2018) https://www.tuc.org.uk/blogs/thousands-low-pai d-retail-workers-are-getting-stuck-not-getting

• Jun Hou, Stephen Gelb and Linda Calabrese, *The Shift in Manufacturing Employment in China, background paper,* (Supporting Economic Transformation, August, 2017) https://set.odi.org/wp-content/uploads/2017/08/SE T-China_Shift-of-Manufacturing-Employment-1.pdf

• International Labour Organization (ILO) *Activist welcome progress towards eradication of forced labour, child labour in Uzbekistan.* Press release (April 3, 2019) https://www.ilo.org/global/about-the-ilo/newsroo m/news/WCMS_681780/lang--en/index.htm

• Jongeneel, R.; Gonzalez-Martinez, A. *EU Dairy after the Quota Abolition: Inelastic Asymmetric Price Responsiveness and Adverse Milk Supply during Crisis Time.* (Agriculture, 2022), *12*, 1985.

• Annie Kelly, *46 million people living as slaves, latest global index reveals.* In The Guardian, (June 1, 2016) https://www.theguardian.com/global-development/2016/j un/01/46-million-people-living-as-slaves-latest-global-ind ex-reveals-russell-crowe

• Herbert Klein, *The Atlantic Slave Trade to 1650.* In *Tropical Babylons: Sugar and the Making of the Atlantic World,*

1450-1680. Stuart B. Schwartz (ed.) (Chapel Hill: University of North Carolina Press, 2004) pg. 201-236

- Alex Knapp, *The Seduction Of The Exponential Curve*. In Forbes, (Nov. 17, 2011) https://www.forbes.com/sites/alexknapp/2011/11/17/the-seduction-of-the-exponential-curve/?sh=6b12c93f2480

- Steve Kreis, *Lecture 17: The Origins of the Industrial Revolution in England*. In The History Guide, (Feb. 1, 2003) http://www.historyguide.org/intellect/lecture17a.html

- Jacqueline Kubania, *How second-hand clothing donations are creating a dilemma for Kenya*. In The Guardian (Jul 6, 2015) https://www.theguardian.com/world/2015/jul/06/second-hand-clothing-donations-kenya

- Paul Lanoie and George A. Tanguay, *Factors Leading to Green Profitability. 10 case studies*. In Greener Management International, Vol. 31, No. 3. (2000) pg. 39-50. https://www.researchgate.net/profile/Georges-Tanguay/pu blication/263407115_Factors_Leading_to_Green_Profitabilit y/links/58a5c30692851cf0e39baec2/Factors-Leading-to-Gr een-Profitability.pdf

- Josephine Moulds, *Child labour in the fashion supply chain. Where, why and what can be done*. (The Guardian, Jan. 15, 2015) https://labs.theguardian.com/unicef-child-labour/

- Laura T. Murphy, et al., *Laundering Cotton, How Xinjiang cotton is obscured in international supply chains*. (Sheffield, United Kingdom: Sheffield Hallam University Helena Kennedy Centre, 2021) https://www.politico.com/f/?id=0000017d -3164-dddc-a77f-35f7068e0000

- Sonia Naran, *In Laos, Textile Traditions Give Rural Women Economic Independence*. (The New Humanitarian, June 6, 2017) https://deeply.thenewhumanitarian.org/womensadvance

ment/articles/2017/06/06/in-laos-textile-traditions-give-r
ural-women-economic-independence

- Max Nisen, *How Nike Solved Its Sweat-shop Problem.* (Business Insider, May 10, 2013) https://www.businessinsider.com/how-nike-solved -its-sweatshop-problem-2013-5?r=US&IR=T

- Michael I. Norton, Daniel Mochon and Dan Ariely, *The IKEA Effect: When Labor Leads to Love.* In Journal of Consumer Psychology22, No. 3 (July 2012) pg 453-460 https://www.hbs. edu/faculty/Pages/item.aspx?num=41121

- Brian Page and Richard Walker, *From Settlement to Fordism: The agro-industrial revolution of the American Midwest.* In Economic Geography, Vol. 67, No. 4 (Okt, 1991) (281 – 315) https://geography.berkeley.edu/sites/default/files/wa lker_51.pdf

- Elizabeth Paton and Milena Lazazzera, *Inside Italy's Shadow Economy.* In New York Times, (Sept. 20, 2019) https://www.nytimes.com/2018/09/20/fashion/ital y-luxury-shadow-economy.html

- Robert Pollin, Justine Burns and James Heintz, *Global apparel production and sweatshop labour: can raising retail prices finance living wages?* In Cambridge Journal of Economics, Vol. 28, No. 2 (Oxford: Oxford University Press, 2004) pg. 153 – 171 https://www.jstor.org/stable/23602122

- Leslie W. Rabine, *Globalization and the Fashion Industry.* (Love to Know, accessed Okt. 9, 2020) https://womens-fashion.lovetoknow.com/womens -fashion-history/globalization-fashion-industry

- Ulla Ræbild and Karen Marie Hasling, *Sustainable Design Cards: A Learning Tool for Supporting Sustainable Design Strategies.* in: Niinimäki, K (Ed.), Sustainable Fashion in a Circular Economy. (Helsinki: Aalto University, 2018)

- Gerhard Rempel. *The Industrial Revolution.* (Feb. 8, 2003) ht tps://www1.udel.edu/fllt/faculty/aml/201files/IndRev.html

- Tansy Robertson-Fall (sr. ed.) *The role of art in driving systems change, Engaging more people in the circular economy discourse.* (London, Ellen MacArthur foundation 2021) https://ellenmacarthurfoundation.org/articles/the-r ole-of-art-in-driving-systems-change

- Johan Rockström et al., *Planetary Boundaries: Exploring the Safe Operating Space for Humanity.* In, Ecology & Society, Vol. 14, No 2, Art 32 (2019) https://www.ecologyandsociety.org /vol14/iss2/art32/

- Walter R. Stahel, *The Circular Economy,* in Nature, 531, 435-438 (March 23, 2016) https://www.nature.com/article s/531435a

- David Teather, *Nike Lists abuses at Asian Factories.* The Guardian, (April 14, 2005) https://www.theguardian.com/ business/2005/apr/14/ethicalbusiness.money

- Frans Timmermans et al. *Weg mit der Wegwerfmentalitat.* In Die Zeit (May 28, 2015) https://www.zeit.de/wirtschaft/2015-05/umweltschutz-kli mawandel-recycling?utm_referrer=https%3A%2F%2Fwww .google.com%2F

- Danielle Treadwell et al. *What is Organic?* (eOrganic, Jan. 22, 2009) https://eorganic.org/node/3498

- Robert E. Ulanowics et al. *Quantifying sustainability: resilience, efficiency, and the return of information theory.* In Ecological Complexity Vol. 6, (2009) Pg 27-36 https://wtf.tw/r ef/ulanowicz.pdf

- Marjorie van Elven, *People do not wear at least 50 percent of their wardrobes, says study.* In FashionUnited (August 16, 2   0   1   8   )

https://fashionunited.uk/news/fashion/people-do-not-we
ar-at-least-50-percent-of-their-wardrobes-according-to-st
udy/2018081638356

- Harrison Wavell, *How History has forged a path to a circular economy.* (London: Ellen LacArthur Foundation, July 19, 2021) https://ellenmacarthurfoundation.org/articles/how-history-has-forged-the-path-to-a-circular-economy

- Mike Werner et al., *The role of safe chemistry and healthy materials in unlocking the circular economy.* (Google & Ellen MacArthur Foundation) https://www.vox.com/the-goods/2020/1/27/2108010 7/fashion-environment-facts-statistics-impact

- Alden Wicker, *Fashion has a misinformation problem. That's bad for the environment.* At Vox (Jan 31, 2020) https://www.vox.com/the-goods/2020/1/27/210801 07/fashion-environment-facts-statistics-impact

- Alden Wicker, *The pandemic lays bare just how futile conscious consumerisme is.* At Ecoasia (April 17, 2020) https://blog.ecosia.org/covid-and-conscious-consumerism/

- Sue Wilkes, *A (Working) Woman's Place, As the Industrial Revolution wrought widespread social changes, female cotton industry workers' lives changed dramatically.* Published in History Today, Volume 67 Issue 5 (June 2017) https://www.historytoday.com/working-woman's-place

Reports

- Alexandre Kossoy et al., *Carbon Pricing Watch.* (Washington DC.: World Bank, 2015) https://openknowledge.worldbank.org/handle/10986/21986

- Anne Lally, *Climbing the Ladder to Living Wages, An Update on FWF's Living Wage research 2011 – 2022* (Amsterdam: Fair

Wear Foundation, 2012)

- Archives parlementaires, *Déclaration des Droits de l'Homme et du Citoyen*. le série, tome VIII, , p. 431) https://www.legifrance.gouv.fr/contenu/menu/droit-natio nal-en-vigueur/constitution/declaration-des-droits-de-l-h omme-et-du-citoyen-de-1789

- Archives parlementaires, *Déclaration des Droits de l'Homme et du Citoyen*. le série, tome VIII, , p. 459.

- CARE, *Guidelines: Apparel Industry Response to Violence and Harassment in the Workplace.* https://www.care.org/news-and-stories/resources/guidelin es-apparel-industry-response-to-violence-and-harassmen t-in-the-workplace/ (June 7, 2021)

- CARE, *Made by Women, Impact Report 2020* (Care, 2021) https://www.care.org/wp-content/uploads/2021/03 /MbW_Impact-report_2020_FINAL.pdf

- CARE, *Preventing Violence and Harassment at Work.* https://www.care.org/our-work/education-and-work/dignif ied-work/preventing-violence-and-harassment-at-work/

- CARE, *Women Take the Lead.* https://www.care.org/our-work/education-and-wor k/dignified-work/empowering-women-to-take-the-lead

- Centre for Sustainable Fashion *Factsheet, Agenda.* (London: University of the Arts London, 2018) https://www.sustaina ble-fashion.com

- Centre for Sustainble Fashion, Fashion Futures 2030 (London: University of the Arts London, 2018) https://www.sus tainable-fashion.com/fashion-futures-2030

- Centre for well-being, Jody Aked et al. Five ways to wellbeing. (London: New Economics Foundation,

2008) https://neweconomics.org/uploads/files/five-ways
-to-wellbeing-1.pdf

- China Labour Watch, *Ted Case Study, Nike: Nike Shoes and Child Labour in Pakistan.* (New York: Chinalaborwatch, Nov. 4, 2010) https://ecommons.cornell.edu/bitstream/handle/1813/1012 27/CLW_2010_Report_China_Ted_Nike.pdf?sequence=1&is Allowed=y

- CFDA, Domenica Leibowitz et al., *Guide to Sustainable Strategies.* (Council of Fashion Designers of America, 2019) https://s3.amazonaws.com/cfda.f.mrhenry.be/2019/ 01/CFDA-Guide-to-Sustainable-Strategies_16.pdf

- CFDA, Kevin Bass and Marc Karimzadeh (ed.), *KPI Design Kit, A Sustainable Strategies Playbook for Measurable Change.* (Council of Fashion Designers of America, 2019) https://s3.amazonaws.com/cfda.f.mrhenry.be/2019/ 10/CFDA-KPI-Design-Kit-HIGHRES.pdf

- Clean Clothing Campaign, *Made by Women. Gender, The global garment industry and the movement for women workers' rights.* (Clean Clothes Campaign, 2005)

- Ecopreneur.eu, *Circular Fashion Advocacy. A strategy towards a circular fashion industry in Europe.* (European Sustainable business federation, 2019) https://ecopreneur.eu/wp-content/uploads/2019/03 /EcoP-Circular-Fashion-Advocacy-Report-28-3-19.pdf

- Ecopreneur.eu,*Circular Fashion and Textile Producing Countries. A first inventory of the potential impact of an EU circular fashion industry on non-European countries.* (European Sustainable business federation, 2020) https://ecopreneur.eu/wp-content/uploads/2020/02/Ecopr eneurEU-Research-Note-on-Circular-Fashion-Impacts-26 -2-2020.pdf

- Edward Langley, Stefan Durkacs and Simona Tanase (Ipsos Mori) *Clothing longevity and measuring active use* (Oxon: WRAP, 2013) https://wrap.org.uk/sites/default/files/2021-04/Clothing%20Longevity%20Report.pdf

- Eli Woolery, *Design Thinking Handbook*, DesignBetter.co by InVision, https://www.designbetter.co/design-thinking

- Ellen MacArthur Foundation, *A new textiles economy: Redesigning fashion's future.* (London: Ellen MacArthur Foundation, 2018) http://www.ellenmacarthurfoundation.org/publications

- Ellen MacArthur Foundation, *Financing the circular economy. Capturing the opportunity.* (London: Ellen MacArthur Foundation, 2020) https://ellenmacarthurfoundation.org/financing-the-circular-economy-capturing-the-opportunity

- Ellen MacArthur Foundation & McKinsey Center for Business and Environment. *Growth within: A circular economy vision for a competitive Europe.* (Jun 1, 2015) https://ellenmacarthurfoundation.org/growth-within-a-circular-economy-vision-for-a-competitive-europe

- Ellen MacArthur Foundation & IDEO, *The circular design guide.* (London: Ellen MacArthur Foundation, 2018) https://www.circulardesignguide.com

- Ellen MacArthur Foundation, *Towards a Circular Economy, business rationales for an accelerated transition.* (London, Ellen MacArthur Foundation, 2015) https://ellenmacarthurfoundation.org/towards-a-circular-economy-business-rationale-for-an-accelerated-transition

- European Environment Agency, *Overview of the use of landfill taxes in Europe. Waste.* (Feb.18, 2015) https://www.eea.europa.eu/soer/2015/countries-comparison/waste

- European Institute for Gender Equality. Concepts and Definitions. (2019) https://eige.europa.eu/gender-mainstreami ng/concepts-and-definitions

- Fashion for Good, *C2C Certified tm "How-To" Guide* (Amsterdam, Fashion For Good, 2017) https://fashionforgood.com/wp-content/uploads/2 017/04/C2C-How-To-Guide_v1.03.pdf

- Fashion Revolution, *Fashion Transparency Index 2019* (London: Fashion Revolution, 2019) https://issuu.com/fashionr evolution/docs/fti_2022

- Fashion Revolution, *Garment Worker Diaries.* (London: Fashion Revolution, 2018) https://workerdiaries.org/our-purpo se/

- Global Living Wage, *Introducing "Understanding Gender Pay Gaps around the World"* (June 17, 2021) https://globallivingwage.org/announcements/introducing -understanding-gender-pay-gaps-around-the-world/

- GLOBE, M. Nachmany et al. *The GLOBE Climate Legislation Study: A Review of Climate Change Legislation in 66 Countries. Fourth Edition.* (London: GLOBE International and the Grantham Research Institute, London School of Economics, 2014) https://www.lse.ac.uk/granthaminstitute/wp-conte nt/uploads/2014/03/Globe2014.pdf

- Greenpeace, *Dirty Laundry, Unravelling the corporate connections to toxic water pollution in China* (Amsterdam: Greenpeace International, 2011) https://www.greenpeace.org/static/planet4-international -stateless/2011/07/2303cc74-dirty-laundry-12pages.pdf

- House of Commons Environmental Audit Committee, *Fixing Fashion: clothing consumption and sustainability.* Sixteenth Report of Session 2017-2019 (London: Parliamentary House of Commons, 2019) https://publications.parliament.uk/pa/

cm201719/cmselect/cmenvaud/1952/report-summary.html

- Human Rights Watch, *Combating Sexual Harassment in the Garment Industry* (Human Rights Watch, Feb. 12, 2019) https://www.hrw.org/news/2019/02/12/combating -sexual-harassment-garment-industry

- Ibis world. *Global biggest Industries by Employment in 2023.* https://www.ibisworld.com/global/industry-trends/ biggest-industries-by-employment/

- IDEO, *The Field Guide to Human-Centered Design.* (San Francisco: IDEO, 2015) https://www.designkit.org/resources/1

- Imram Amed et al., *The State of Fashion 2017* (London,: McKinsey&Company & BOF, 2016)

- Imram Amed et al., *The State of Fashion 2022* (London,: McKinsey&Company & BOF, 2021)

- Imram Amed et al., *The State of Fashion 2023* (London,: McKinsey&Company & BOF, 2022)

- Institute for Sustainability Leadership (CISL), Shift, Business Fights Poverty and University of Cambridge. J. Nelson, et al. *The case for living wages: how paying living wages improves business performance and tackles poverty.* (Cambridge: Univeristy of Cambridge, May 16, 2022) https://www.evidensia.eco/resources/2117/the-case-for-livi ng-wages-how-paying-living-wages-improves-business-p erformance-and-tackles-poverty/

- International Labour Organization (ILO) & Walk Free Foundation, *Global Estimate of Modern Slavery, forced labour and forced marriage.* (Geneva: ILO, 2017) https://www.ilo.org/wcmsp5/groups/public/---dgreports/ ---dcomm/documents/publication/wcms_575479.pdf

- International Labour Organization (ILO) & Walk Free

Foundation, *Methodology of the global estimates of modern slavery: Forced labour and forced marriage.* (Geneva: ILO, 2017) https://www.ilo.org/wcmsp5/groups/public/---ed_n orm/---ipec/documents/publication/wcms_586127.pdf

• International Labour Organization (ILO) & Walk Free Foundation, *Global Estimates of Child Labour. Results and Trends, 2012 – 2016* (Geneva: ILO, 2017) https://www.ilo.org/wcmsp5/groups/public/---dgreports/ ---dcomm/documents/publication/wcms_575499.pdf

• International Labour Organization (ILO), *Uzbek cotton is free from systemic child labour and forced labour.* Press release (March 1, 2022) https://www.ilo.org/global/about-the-ilo/ newsroom/news/WCMS_838396/lang--en/index.html

• International Labour Organization (ILO), *Women at Work, trends 2016.* (Geneva: ILO, 2016) https://www.ilo.org/wcmsp5/groups/public/---dgreports/ ---dcomm/---publ/documents/publication/wcms_457317.p df

• IPCC, 2019: *Climate Change and Land: an IPCC special report on climate change, desertification, land degradation, sustainable l a n d management, food security, and greenhouse gas fluxes in terrestriale cosystems*[P.R.Shukla,J.Skea,E.CalvoBuendia,V.Masson-Del motte, H.-O. Poïrtner, D. C. Roberts, P. Zhai, R. Slade, S. Connors, R. van Diemen, M. Ferrat, E. Haughey, S. Luz, S. Neogi, M. Pathak, J. Petzold, J. Portugal Pereira, P. Vyas, E. Huntley, K. Kissick, M. Belkacemi, J. Malley, (eds.)]. In press. https://www.ipcc.ch/site/assets/uploads/2019/11/SRCCL-Fu ll-Report-Compiled-191128.pdf

• IPCC, 2022: Summary for Policymakers [H.-O.Poïrtner, D.C .Roberts, E.S.Poloczanska, K.Mintenbeck, M.Tignor, A. Ale- grïá, M. Craig, S. Langsdorf, S. Lošchke, V. Moîler, A. Okem (eds.)]. In: *Climate Change 2022: Impacts, Adaptation and Vul-*

nerability. Contribution of Working Group II to the Sixth Assessment Report of the Intergovernmental Panel on Climate Change [H.-O.Pörtner, D.C.Roberts, M.Tignor, E.S. Poloczanska, K.Mintenbeck, A.Alegría, M.Craig, S. Langsdorf, S. Löschke, V. Moller, A. Okem, B. Rama (eds.)]. Cambridge University Press, Cambridge, UK and New York, NY, USA, pp. 3–33, doi:10.1017/9781009325844.001. https://www.ipcc.ch/report/ar6/wg2/downloads/report/I PCC_AR6_WGII_SummaryForPolicymakers.pdf

• Jonas Eder-Hansen et al., *Pulse of the Fashion Industry 2017* (n.d.: Global Fashion Agenda & The Boston Consulting Group, 2017)

• Jonas Eder-Hansen et al., *Pulse of the Fashion Industry 2018* (n.d.: Global Fashion Agenda & The Boston Consulting Group, 2018)

• Jonas Eder-Hansen et al., *Pulse of the Fashion Industry 2019* (n.d.: Global Fashion Agenda & The Boston Consulting Group, 2019)

• Learning Journey, *Circular Design*. https://www.circulardes ignguide.com/resources

• Liv Simpliciano et al., *Fashion Transparency Index, 2022 Edition* (n.d.: Fashion Revolution, 2022)

• McDonough Braungart Design Chemistry, *Material Health Assessment Methodology*. (Charlottesville: Cradle to Cradle products Innovation Institute, Last Revision, Feb. 2022) https://cdn.c2ccertified.org/resources/certification/standar d/MTD_Material_Health_Assessment_FINAL_021522.pdf

• McDonough Braungart Design Chemistry, *Cradle to Cradle CertifiedR Version 4.0, Product Standard*. (Charlottesville: Cradle to Cradle products Innovation Institute, 2021) https://cdn.c2ccertified.org/resources/certification/s tandard/STD_C2C_Certified_V4.0_FINAL_031621.pdf

- Somo, *Fact Sheet; Child labour in the textile & garment industry.* (Amsterdam: Stichting Onderzoek Multinationale Ondernemingen, 2014) https://www.somo.nl/wp-content/uploads/2014/03/Fact-Sheet-child-labour-Focus-on-the-role-of-buying-companies.pdf

- Somo, Flawed Fabrics, *The abuse of girls and women workers in the South Indian textile industry.* (Amsterdam, SOMO, 2014) http://www.indianet.nl/pdf/FlawedFabrics.pdf

- The Danish Institute for Human Rights, *Freedom of association and collective bargaining.* (Copenhagen: The Danish Institute for Human Rights, accessed Feb. 8, 2023) https://biz.sdg.humanrights.dk/salient-issue/freedom-of-association-and-collective-bargaining

- UCLA Charter *What is Sustainability? Sustainability is the balance between the environment, equity, and economy.* (Los Angeles: Univeristy of California, 2019) (https://www.sustain.ucla.edu/what-is-sustainability/

- UNICEF, *The United Nations Convention on the Rights of the Child.* Entry into force September 2, 1990. (London: Unicef, 2010) https://downloads.unicef.org.uk/wp-content/uploads/2010/05/UNCRC_united_nations_convention_on_the_rights_of_the_child.pdf

- United Nations, *Dispatch: Only Six Countries In the World Have Full Gender Equality in the Work Place.* (New York: United Nations, Mar 8, 2019) https://www.undispatch.com/only-six-countries-in-the-world-that-have-full-gender-equality-in-the-work-place/

- United Nations, *Women: Equal pay for work of equal value.* (New York: United Nations, 2019) https://www.unwomen.org/en/news/in-focus/csw61/equal-pay

- United Nations, *World population prospects 2022, summary of results.* (New York: United Nations, 2022) https://www.un.org/development/desa/pd/sites/www.un.o rg.development.desa.pd/files/wpp2022_summary_of_resul ts.pdf

- Walk Free Foundation, *The Global Slavery Index 2018.* https://www.globalslaveryindex.org/resources/dow nloads/#gsi-2018

- WORLD Policy Analysis Centre, *Preventing gender-based workplace discrimination and sexual harassment: new data on 193 countries.* (Los Angeles: WORLD 2017) https://www.glo balslaveryindex.org/resources/downloads/#gsi-2018

- WRAP, *Design for Longevity, Guidance on increasing the active life of clothing.* (Oxon: May 2013) https://wrap.org.uk/resou rces/report/design-extending-clothing-life

- WRAP, *Sustainable clothing. A practical guide to enhancing clothing durability and quality.* (Oxon: WRAP, 2017)

- WRAP, *Valuing our Clothes: the cost of UK fashion* (Oxon: WRAP, 2017)

- WWF, *Soil Erosion and Degradation, overview, causes, impacts.* https://www.worldwildlife.org/threats/soil-erosion -and-degradation

- Quantis, *Measuring Fashion, Environmental Impact of the Global Apparel and Footwear Industries Study.* (2018) https://quantis.com/wp-content/uploads/2018/03/measuri ngfashion_globalimpactstudy_full-report_quantis_cwf_201 8a.pdf

Documentary

- Foreign correspondent, *Dead White Man's Clothes* producer Alison McClymont (ABC News, 2021) https://www.you tube.com/watch?v=bB3kuuBPVys based on the immersive multimedia research project: *Dead White Man's Clothes*. Executive director Liz Ricketts (2016 – Present) https://theor. org/work

- Short movie, *Design Q&A, Questions by Mme. L. Amic. Answers by Charles Eames1972,* on the occasion of the exhibition "Qu'est ce que le design" at the Musée des Arts Décoratifs, Palais de Louvre. (1972, Charles and Ray Eames. 1992, 1993 Lucia Eames Demetrios dba Eames Office.) https://www.y outube.com/watch?v=bmgxDCujTUw

Printed in Great Britain
by Amazon

23741301R00131